QUESTIONS OF POSSIBILITY

QUESTIONS OF POSSIBILITY

Contemporary Poetry and Poetic Form

DAVID CAPLAN

OXFORD
UNIVERSITY PRESS

Oxford   New York

Auckland   Bangkok   Buenos Aires   Cape Town   Chennai
Dar es Salaam   Delhi   Hong Kong   Istanbul   Karachi   Kolkata
Kuala Lumpur   Madrid   Melbourne   Mexico City   Mumbai   Nairobi
São Paulo   Shanghai   Taipei   Tokyo   Toronto

Copyright © 2005 by Oxford University Press, Inc.

Published by Oxford University Press, Inc.
198 Madison Avenue, New York, New York 10016

www.oup.com

Oxford is a registered trademark of Oxford University Press

Library of Congress Cataloging-in-Publication Data
Caplan, David, 1947–
Questions of possibility : contemporary poetry and poetic form /
David Caplan
p. cm.
Includes index.
ISBN 0-19-516957-3
1. American poetry—20th century—History and criticism.
2. American poetry—21st century—History and criticism. 3. English language—
Versification. 4. Literary form. 5. Poetics. I. Title.
PS325.C37 2004
811'.509—dc22   2004002168

1 3 5 7 9 8 6 4 2

Printed in the United States of America
on acid-free paper

ACKNOWLEDGMENTS

I am indebted to the poets I discuss who read chapters of the book in manuscript: Charles Bernstein, Rafael Campo, Sam Gwynn, Dana Gioia, H. L. Hix, Jennifer Moxley, and Marilyn Nelson. Heather Dubrow, William Logan, Jeredith Merrin, and Heather Love gave me helpful suggestions on individual chapters, drawing from their formidable knowledge of the subjects I consider. Conversations with Dick Davis, Ted Genoways, Randall Mann, and C. Dale Young have deepened my understanding of poetic form. Gena McKinley read this entire manuscript, giving me excellent advice. Rick Huard patiently copyedited my endnotes and Carolyn C. Sherayku prepared the index.

I remain deeply indebted to my family: my brother, parents, grandmother, and sister-in-law. "Support" only inadequately conveys the depth and variety of encouragement they have provided me during my years of study and research. Thanks also are due to John Picker, June Griffin, Mara Amster, Kevin Clarke, Nelson Tarr, Janey Meeks, Alex Pitofsky, Mike Esler, Mark McWilliams, and Marty Hipsky, whose friendship made this book possible.

Several of these chapters have been presented at conferences or given as talks. I would like to thank the members of the University of Michigan's "Forum on Form," especially organizer Richard Cureton, for the warm hospitality during my visit, and the other participants in Ohio Wesleyan University's faculty seminar, run by Jeff Nunemacher.

I also benefited from the comments received during my presentations at the Northeast Modern Language Association convention and the annual conventions of the Modern Language Association.

In many respects, this book is a product of the "Exploring Form and Narrative Conference" held annually at West Chester University, where I presented several chapters. This book continues conversations began at that conference. Organizers Michael Peich and Dana Gioia have created a lively, welcoming environment where prosody can be discussed and disagreements honored. That conference also introduced me to the work of two younger poets, which this book discusses.

I began this project at the University of Virginia and finished it at Ohio Wesleyan University. I am grateful for the intellectual sustenance and financial support that both institutions offered. A Yalden-Thompson Summer Fellowship from the University of Virginia's Society of Fellows gave me the time to finish the dissertation while Ohio Wesleyan has generously provided me several forms of support, including special scholarly leave time and research fellowships. Jahan Ramazani, Stephen Cushman, and Larry Buchard read the work in its entirety and offered useful suggestions and probing questions. My students have helped me to clarify the pedagogical implications of the ideas my research raised. I am grateful for the opportunity to discuss poetry and issues of poetic form with them.

I am truly fortunate to have as my editor Elissa Morris, a model of efficiency and good cheer, ably assisted by Jeremy Lewis. The suggestions offered by James Longenbach and Annie Finch, whose identities were revealed after the manuscript's acceptance, helped to polish the manuscript.

This book is dedicated to Ralph Cohen for his wise counsel.

CREDITS

CONTENTS

Introduction: On Claimed Verse Forms   3

1. "The Age of the Sestina"   17

2. "In that Thicket of Bitter Roots": The Ghazal in America   43

3. When a Form Comes Out of the Closet   61

4. Why Not the Heroic Couplet?   87

5. On the Contemporary Ballad   105

Conclusion: Prosody after the Poetry Wars   127

Notes   139

Index   159

QUESTIONS OF POSSIBILITY

INTRODUCTION

ON CLAIMED VERSE FORMS

The challenge to contemporary poetry would seem
to be a pair of unhappy alternatives: either to contrive
new schemes of empirically meaningful repetition that
reflect and—more importantly—transmit the color of
contemporary experience; or to recover schemes that have
reflected the experience of the past. To do the first would
be to imply that contemporary experience has a pattern,
a point that most post-Christian thinkers would deny. To
do the second would be to suggest that the past can be
recaptured, to suggest that the intolerable fractures and
dislocations of modern history have not really occurred
at all, or, what is worse, to suggest that they may have
occurred but that poetry should act as if they have not
... [W]e yield now to the one demand, now to the other,
producing at times a formless and artistically incoherent
reflection—accurate in its way—of some civil or social or
psychological reality, and at times a shapely and coherent
work of art which is necessarily an inexact report on the
state of affairs, not to mention the state of language and
meaning and coherence, in our time.

—Paul Fussell, *Poetic Meter and Poetic Form*

CONTEMPORARY METRICAL VERSE SURPRISES MANY LEARNED READERS
simply by existing. For all the reasons that Fussell summarizes and
for a great number more, much of the liveliest recent scholarship
concludes that literary and cultural history dooms this poetry to failure,
irrelevance, or political and aesthetic conservatism. "[T]he pentameter
is a dead form," Antony Easthope notes, "and its continued use . . .
is in the strict sense reactionary."[1] Many other commentators agree,
calling contemporary "neo-formalism" "a dangerous nostalgia," "the
new conservatism in American poetry," and a Reaganite "return to old
values." Despite these admonishments, poets continue to write metrical
verse; during the last two decades especially, a wide variety of American

poets have turned to these forms.[2] Oddly, the insults remain more widely known than the poems they attack.

This study reexamines contemporary metrical verse, the poetry that would seem to pursue the second of Fussell's "unhappy alternatives." Yet it does nothing of the sort. Instead, the poets I will discuss have developed possibilities outside these two options and the familiar set of oppositions that underlie them: the choice between "new schemes" that "transmit" "the intolerable fractures and dislocations of modern history" and older verse forms that seek merely to "recapture" a more coherent past.

Anthologies of postmodern poetry and critical discussions typically exclude metrical verse because it advances, in two anthologists' characterization, a "retrograde poetics."[3] When more broadly considered, though, postmodern art resists the false choice between "new schemes" and "the schemes . . . of the past." The postmodern novel, for example, has often been characterized by its interest in historical modes and techniques, including the romance, the picaresque, and the early English novel's mixture of genres. As Milan Kundera has noted, this fiction "rehabilitat[es]" earlier "novelistic principles." Its aim is not "a return to this or that retro style"; instead, it seeks "to give the novel its *entire* historical experience for a grounding."[4]

The commitment to this ideal is also evident in recently developed artforms. Just as Bill Viola's earlier video/sound installation *The Greeting* borrows from Jacopo Pontormo's sixteenth-century painting *The Visitation*, Viola's *Going Forth by Day* draws from Giotto's Scrovegni Chapel fresco series, which Viola calls "one of the greatest works of installation art in the world."[5] Recorded in high-definition video, *Going Forth by Day* uses Renaissance framing techniques to depict a terribly contemporary moment. One screen stays focused on a city building whose neoclassical doorway and shuttered windows provide a symmetrical background to the various actors who move in and out of the shot. In an eerie anticipation of the events of September 11, the scene suddenly changes, depicting (in Viola's words) the "panic [that] ensues as individuals rush to save themselves. . . . Individual lives and personal possessions are arbitrarily chosen to be lost in the process" (Viola, *Going Forth*, 38). Torrents of water inexplicably pour from the building whose inhabitants desperately flee the disaster. "[W]hen the future arrives, this is how it looks," the science writer James Gleick notes. "It comes all mixed up like a junkyard, the old and the new jumbled together."[6] Demonstrating this idea, Viola elegantly "jumbles" fresco conventions with cutting-edge technology.

Rejecting the notion that metrical verse cannot express contemporary existence, crucial figures in the development of postmodernity specifically advocated metrical technique. In a 1985 article devoted to the subject, Primo Levi promoted rhyme's "spontaneous return." As Levi argued, rhyme inspires, not hinders, formal experimentation. "The restriction of rhyme," Levi asserted, "obliges the poet to resort to the unpredictable: compels him to invent, to 'find'; and to enrich his lexicon with unusual terms; bend his syntax; in short, to innovate."[7] Jorge Luis Borges similarly called an interest in metrical technique part of an aspiring poet's necessary "curiosity." During a 1971 visit to Columbia University, Borges advised creative writing students to follow his example and write "classical forms of verse," although the students "may think of [such forms] as being old-fashioned." When an audience member confessed, "I can't imagine writing sonnets or rhyming couplets," Borges replied, "I am very sorry."[8]

To call Borges a "postmodern" prose writer and a "traditional" poet overlooks the crucial point: that this exemplar of postmodernity saw no contradiction in writing sonnets and fables, rhyming couplets and picaresque tales, rehabilitating the "classical forms" of poetry and of prose fiction. As he reminded his audience, he wrote free verse as well as sonnets and enjoyed reading poetry in both forms. Speaking of Whitman's *Leaves of Grass* and "a sonnet by Shakespeare or Wordsworth or Keats or Yeats," Borges remarked, "There is no need to like one and discard the other, since you can keep both." Indeed, Borges called "the question" of which is better "meaningless" (Borges, *Borges on Writing*, 70).

Vibrant, diverse, and contentious, contemporary poetry demands the catholicity that Borges advocates. His sensible comments capture many readers' tastes, as they enjoy poetry that literary criticism separates into different groups. (This lack of partisanship makes the poetry recommendation lists that amazon.com customers post livelier than most college syllabi.) To write more personally, Borges's remarks speak to my own experience. While some of my favorite poets use metrical technique, many do not. I admire Marilyn Nelson's "new formalist" poems and Charles Bernstein's "nude formalist" parodies. Following Borges, I refuse to "like one and discard the other" because to do so would severely limit the pleasure and wisdom that contemporary poetry offers.

To understand contemporary poetry, we need to range from its well-worn debates to visit, for instance, the Massachusetts Museum of Contemporary Art (MASS MoCA). Opened in 1999, the museum renovated an abandoned nineteenth-century mill complex into the world's largest center of contemporary art. The mill's sprawling, idiosyncratic arrangement and large open spaces—what the museum's director calls its "legitimate architecture of accretion, and the grace of an inherited gift"—provides a unique forum for innovative work, such as installations, video art, and sound environments.[9] Simeon Bruner elaborates in his architect's statement: "MASS MoCA retains what is historic, provides an exciting way to use the new, and winds up creating a single new piece that is both old and new at the same time. There is no conflict between the two, and they enhance one another seamlessly" (Trainer, *MASS MoCA*, 113). Instead of opposing the "new" and "old," "innovative" and "historic," Bruner explores how the contemporary moment might carefully reconsider preexisting styles and forms, not repudiate them. "There is no conflict between the two, and they enhance one another seamlessly"; this hope also inspires many of the poets I will consider.

This study departs from most discussions of contemporary metrical verse in that it is less interested in poetic movements than the movement of poetic forms. Instead of concentrating my efforts on promoting or dismissing certain schools, I consider the particular forms that contemporary poets favor and those they neglect. These choices reveal both the poets' ambitions and their limits, the new possibilities they discover and the traditions they find unimaginable. I focus on five especially suggestive verse forms, five points to trace the particular contours of contemporary metrical verse and poetic culture: the sestina, ghazal, love sonnet, heroic couplet, and ballad.

Such forms are often called "traditional," although many remain eccentric within English-language literary history, and "given" or "received" as if poets passively accept them. Yet Adrienne Rich's observation about education is also true of poetic forms: they must be claimed.[10] Unlike certain moments in the eighteenth century or during the Renaissance, the contemporary era features no obligatory verse form, no structure that any respectable poet "must" write. The contemporary poet instead enjoys a wide variety of available poetic forms. When composing he or she must claim one: choose it from a host of possibilities. This process lacks the passivity that "given," "received," and, to a lesser degree, "traditional" imply.

Written by the last great American poet to promote his work as "traditional," T. S. Eliot's "Reflections on 'Vers Libre'" suggests why we need a more precise vocabulary to discuss poetic form. "'Blank verse,'" Eliot notes in one of the least discussed passages, "is the only accepted rhymeless verse in English—the inevitable iambic pentameter. The English ear is (or was) more sensitive to the music of the verse and less dependent upon the recurrence of identical sounds in this metre than in any other."[11] Just after he calls "iambic pentameter" "inevitable," Eliot withdraws the claim. "The English ear is *(or was)*" more attuned to this meter than to "any other" (my italics). This telling qualification marks an important historical shift; it acknowledges that modernity had removed iambic pentameter from its privileged status. Poets continued to write in the meter, but it no longer reigned supreme.

No meter has since risen to replace iambic pentameter as "the only acceptable" option, not even free verse, although it did achieve a near-hegemony in the late sixties and early seventies. The plurality of alternatives that contemporary poets encounter—a situation Eliot would liken to anarchy—stretches the term "traditional" until it describes nearly any preexisting form a contemporary poet might use. (And sometimes even more: an anthology of "Contemporary American Poetry in Traditional Forms" includes what its editors call "'new traditional' forms," that is, verse forms that the featured writers invented.[12]) This situation makes the poets' formal choices both highly suggestive and nearly impossible to anticipate. In 1919 Eliot predicted that all that was needed was "the coming of a Satirist . . . to prove that the heroic couplet has lost none of its edge." "As for the sonnet," he added, "I am not so sure" (Eliot, *Selected Prose*, 36). Since then, though, the sonnet has flourished much more than the couplet. Other poets had not accurately forecasted their own metrical choices, let alone larger formal trends.[13] Lacking a stable sense of the culture's poetic "tradition," modern predictions about poetic form achieved a near-perfect consistency; they almost always turned out to be wrong.

Exploiting this situation, contemporary poets claim forms by using techniques thought to be in conflict, creating, as Simeon Bruner wrote of the MASS MoCA, "a single new piece that is both old and new at the same time." The results mystify readers wedded to anachronistic notions of literary influence. When asked about recent trends in poetry, Jorie Graham marveled at the various techniques that younger poets employ. "They're managing," Graham commented,

> a synthesis of the many—oftentimes balkanized—aesthetic devices the generation previous to them developed. . . . It fascinates me, worries me, and in many ways delights me—especially as a poet who has witnessed such great antagonisms between differing aesthetic schools—to see them sample and synthesize and invent without feeling the need to be accountable to the beliefs that gave birth to those voices and styles they imitate.[14]

This "synthesis" thrills and unnerves Graham because she believes the younger generation enjoys a new freedom, one that she and her peers lacked. Instead of negotiating the "great antagonisms between differing aesthetic schools," the younger poets "sample and synthesize and invent." When these poets discuss literary technique, though, they employ very different terms. Martin Corless-Smith, for instance, reverses Graham's assumptions. While this blending of lessons learned from "differing aesthetic schools" strikes her as almost shockingly bold, he matter-of-factly describes it as what artists are "supposed to do." Speaking for his contemporaries, Corless-Smith comments, "We . . . sit on a lot of shoulders. Art is I suppose a mixture of conservatism and revolution. I wouldn't write how I do if I hadn't read Middle English lyrics, or Wordsworth or the Beano or Susan Howe." Demonstrating Corless-Smith's appreciation of what he calls "complex samples of influence," his masque, "The Garden. A Theophany or ECCO HOME a dialectical lyric," takes part of its title from Susan Howe's misprint of Nietzsche's *Ecce Homo*. "The Garden" claims the masque form, drawing from and revising its conventions to include techniques associated with contemporary avant-garde verse.[15]

   Like all powerful new literature, such vital poetry compels a reexamination of the previous generation's work. Following the hints that it offers, we must remain alert to the inspiration that shrewd writers have found in seemingly unlikely sources, even amid a "balkanized" literary landscape. Toward this goal, I will explore how Donald Justice, often labeled "an academic formalist," borrowed composition methods from John Cage, a central figure in postwar and contemporary avant-gardist movements. Also, as another chapter will show, certain gay and lesbian poets have dominated the art of the love sonnet, reviving this most "traditional" form by drawing sustenance from queer theory, scholarship's most "radical" field.

By highlighting this commerce between allegedly antagonistic practices, between prosody and "theory," "traditional" and "experimental" poetry, I hope to move discussion beyond the simple oppositions that often impede discussions of contemporary American verse. This study instead contends that much of the most vital and interesting contemporary metrical verse shows a voracious curiosity, an openness to seemingly incompatible techniques and procedures. These poems stand with, and on the shoulders of, surprising influences. For this reason, I pay close attention to what the authors say and to what their verse forms reveal, attentive to the possibility that the forms the poets claim violate the partisan assertions they express in interviews and in essays.

But why study poetic form at all? Two reasons in particular recommend the subject. First, it obsesses twentieth- and twenty-first-century American poets, who compulsively frame historical and artistic challenges in formal terms. Though hardly unprecedented, this fixation constitutes a defining characteristic of the period's poetic culture. This tendency transcends considerable differences in sensibility and political orientation. Any subject that fascinates poets as different as Adrienne Rich and Donald Justice, T. S. Eliot and Ron Silliman, Marilyn Hacker and John Crowe Ransom demands serious critical attention.

Interest in poetic form has only grown more intense in the last two decades, as contemporary poets have produced an impressive body of literature about prosody. At least two handbooks of prosody have been published recently, along with several collections of essays, and an anthology of verse forms—all written and edited by poets.[16] One title announces prosody to be "the poem's heartbeat"; another considers "the politics of poetic form." Together, these two titles suggest what the wider conversation confirms: that the study of poetic form rewards close attention because even a seemingly minor technical matter such as a poet's eccentric enjambment finely intertwines the aesthetic and the political, the idiosyncratic and the shared.

Second, there are many reasons to believe that our current understanding of poetic form, especially contemporary metrical verse, remains inadequate. Central to this failure is the most familiar set of oppositions I alluded to earlier. Criticism generally frames postwar and contemporary verse as a contest between "experimental" and "traditional" poets. Every decade or so, the terms shift, but the basic opposition remains nearly constant. Read as a rivalry, this division inflects the various postwar and contemporary "poetry wars," raging between the proponents of "the raw" and "the cooked," writers of "open" and "closed" forms, and L=A=N=G=U=A=G=E Writers and new formalists. For at least the last two decades, the most interesting studies of poetic form have tended to focus on the first half of this pair. I have in mind Cary Nelson's *Our Last First Poets*, "a collection of readings of individual poets working in open forms," Charles Bernstein's wonderfully provocative essays, and Marjorie Perloff's groundbreaking work on "the poetics of indeterminacy."[17] If discussed at all, metrical verse is invoked as a neat contrast, a weak opponent quickly dispatched.

These dismissals rest on two problematic assumptions. First, such readings depend on an antagonistic, unnuanced model of literary change, in which a new form of avant-garde writing simply displaces an older one. Martial metaphors are often invoked in order to divide various writers into two warring camps. Second, these claims about the politics of poetic form betray impatience with the mechanics of both politics and poetic form. They assume a straightforward correlation between verse structure and "politics" in its most common meaning. Though William Carlos Williams's rejection of the sonnet as "fascistic" offers an extreme example, it nicely captures a general tendency to see poetic form as a simple reflection of political allegiances.

A poem by Billy Collins, America's poet laureate from 2001 to 2003, more gently illuminates the xenophobia that underpins such pronouncements:

> We do not speak like Petrarch or wear a hat like Spenser
> and it is not fourteen lines
> like furrows in a small, carefully plowed field
> but the picture postcard, a poem on vacation.[18]

Collins's "American Sonnet" drolly expresses a commonplace: that the sonnet remains foreign to American experience. "We" Americans do not write like Italian and English authors. Gerald Stern makes the same point in reverse, titling a recent collection *American Sonnets*. The book's poems are only loosely metrical, do not rhyme, and range from sixteen to twenty-four lines. Like Collins, he uses "American sonnets" as a contradiction in terms. While Collins cites the postcard as the form's truest example, Stern presents free verse.[19]

Such poems cleverly advance a familiar understanding of American literary history that posits the most authentic American artists rebel from Old World traditions and start anew. They slight our country's many fine sonneteers, poets as diverse as Marilyn Hacker, Gwendolyn Brooks, and Robert Frost, implying that they exert an alien influence. They ignore populist verse such as the sonnet that adorns the Statue of Liberty's base, presenting a narrow vision of American and Americanness, where "foreign" poets and verse forms need not apply.

Instead of assigning stable values to poetic forms, we need the patience to trace the forms' shifting movements, as their political and their aesthetic uses accommodate new imperatives and contexts. We must attend to the complications that make poetic forms fascinating.

In 1919, just as Eliot foresaw the sonnet's demise, the members of an all-black railroad dining-room crew wept when a fellow waiter read a sonnet he had just composed, inspired by the summer's race riots and an editor's challenge to address the horrors "like Milton when he wrote 'On the Late Massacre in Piedmont.'"[20] Quickly published, the poem expressed black rage forcefully enough for government officials to denounce it. Senator Henry Cabot Lodge Jr. read it into the *Congressional Record* as a dangerous example of what he called "Negro extremism," just as a Department of Justice investigation "against persons advising anarchy, sedition, and the forcible overthrow of the government" cited the recently published poem with alarm.[21]

The poem's next generation of readers read it very differently. Famously and perhaps apocryphally Winston Churchill is widely reported to have quoted the sonnet to rally England during World War II. Churchill, according to Melvin B. Tolson, "paraded in it before the House of Commons, as if it were the talismanic uniform of His Majesty's field marshal." A white American soldier carried the poem to his death in battle, where it was found among his remains.[22]

Since World War II, the sonnet—and I speak of course of Claude McKay's "If We Must Die"—continued to fascinate readers. Millions of schoolchildren have memorized it. It even made *Time* magazine after a reporter discovered it in the Attica State prison following the September 1971 uprising, the largest penal rebellion in American history. Reading the sonnet as a call to action, the prisoners circulated it to each other, along with banned books by Malcolm X and Bobby Seale. *Time* reproduced the poem's first quatrain, meticulously copied in a prisoner's neat script. Showing far less care, the magazine identified the words as "written by an unknown prisoner, crude but touching in its would-be heroic style."[23] Two issues later, a concerned reader, "Gwendolyn Brooks of Chicago," corrected the error, rebuking *Time's* "poetry specialist," who failed to recognize "one of the most famous poems ever written." Pointedly Brooks concluded her letter by quoting the poem in full:

> If we must die, let it not be like hogs
> Hunted and penned in an inglorious spot,
> While round us bark the mad and hungry dogs,
> Making their mock at our accursed lot.
> If we must die, O, let us nobly die,
> So that our precious blood may not be shed
> In vain; then even the monsters we defy
> Shall be constrained to honor us though dead!
> O, kinsmen! We must meet the common foe!
> Though far outnumbered let us show us brave,
> And for their thousand blows deal one death-blow!
> What though before us lies the open grave?
> Like men we'll face the murderous, cowardly pack,
> Pressed to the wall, dying, but fighting back![24]

Poetic form played shifting roles at the various stages of the poem's reception. By definition a Shakespearean sonnet such as "If We Must Die" employs a host of mnemonic devices; its brevity and rhyming patterns make the poem relatively easy to memorize. Whether or not they could name the form, the prisoners at Attica surely appreciated the fact that "If We Must Die" remained brief enough to smuggle. For a poem to inspire them at crucial moments, the prisoners needed to know it by heart, to quote appropriate lines to themselves and each other. Highly portable and memorable, the sonnet form helped make "If We Must Die" a great prison rebellion poem.

The sonnet form also contributed to the poem's nearly immediate popularity among African American readers a half-century earlier. "If We Must Die" made McKay's career in black America, so much so that he later rued that "the Negro people [who] unanimously hailed me as a poet" on the basis of "that one grand outburst" showed little interest in his other work (McKay, *Long Way from Home*, 31). These readers had no trouble recognizing the sonnet's author and the "we" he spoke for as "black," even though the poem made no overt racial references.[25] The verse form assisted this identification. Several major poets of the Harlem Renaissance, including McKay, Countee Cullen, and James Weldon Johnson, wrote sonnets. Though subsequent literary criticism generally privileges black poets' use of more putatively "black" forms such as the blues and jazz, McKay pursued a well-established strategy when he used what he termed "older traditions" to express his "most lawless and revolutionary passions and moods."[26] His sonnet employed the grand Miltonic rhetoric familiar to many black churches, where ministers sermonized with it. Houston A. Baker Jr. has called this black culture "a world bent on recognizable (rhyme, meter, form, etc.) artistic 'contributions' where familiar structures such as ballads and sonnets presented the greatest 'use.'"[27] In this context, the verse form and rhetoric acted as racial markers.

The sonnet also addressed a decade-old score. McKay started his literary career in Jamaica, his homeland, writing dialect verse. In a memoir he scornfully remembered the local poetry scene:

> Our poets thought it was an excellent thing if they could imitate the English poets. We had poetry societies for the nice people. There were "Browning Clubs," where the poetry of Robert Browning was read but not understood. I had read my poems before many of these societies and the members used to say: "Well, he's very nice and pretty, you know, but he's not a real poet as Browning and Tennyson are poets." I used to think I would show them something. Someday I would write poetry in straight English and amaze and confound them.[28]

Motivated by these slights, "If We Must Die" proved the poet's mastery of the English literary tradition, as he successfully imitated the appropriate models. His technical skill carried more than a hint of defiance, a determination to "amaze and confound" the black anglophiles who misunderstood the very literature they defended. While "If We Must Die" assailed the state of American race relations, circa 1919, its form settled old grudges from the British West Indies. It both rebuked and sustained colonialism's intellectual influence.

These brief episodes in the sonnet's long history resist any single value one might ascribe to the form. Instead, they demonstrate poetic form's ability to claim contradictory political meanings. Because verse form is essentially senseless—an iamb, for instance, merely defines an abstract pattern—it stays open to multifold meanings, to new uses and unexpected inflections. It can express racial solidarity as well as air intraracial grievances; its brevity and technical devices recommend it to prisoners plotting a rebellion, schoolteachers who need a poem to assign, and, perhaps, a Prime Minister fond of Shakespearean cadences. Reviewing McKay's *Selected Poems*, Tolson spoke for many when he charged that McKay's "radicalism was in content—not in form."[29] A form's "radicalism," though, should not be judged so abstractly. Poetic form, like politics itself, relentlessly accommodates local conditions, whether of the Harlem Renaissance, colonial Jamaica, or Leninist Russia, where McKay read "If We Must Die" to Red Army troops, "transformed into a rare instrument and electrified by the great current running through the world" (McKay, *Long Way from Home*, 210). To account for such moments, literary criticism must stay alert to each form's elasticity, vigilant to the uses that verse technique makes of each context and occasion.

Given the prevalent critical bias against metrical verse, my first task is recuperative. For this reason, I begin with the sestina, a much-maligned form, whose popularity is often interpreted as the sign of formal complacency. In English the form entered the twentieth century during the Great Depression, as poets grappled with the dilemma of how to address the day's most pressing social concern but not compose (in Elizabeth Bishop's phrase) "'social conscious' writing."[30] The resulting poems taught younger metrical writers the form's modernity, its ability to confront the age's urgent challenges.

My second chapter considers the ghazal as a case study of how poets import a verse form, revising it to address their own cultural and artistic exigencies. In the late 1960s, Adrienne Rich turned to the ghazal, a canonical form of Persian poetry, in order to construct a poetry of witness. As Black Nationalism and Black Power split from the Civil Rights Movement, her project revealed its fissures and rifts, the oversights and presumptions that ghazals written during the previous decade underscored. Two decades later, Agha Shahid Ali used the same form to reassert the differences Rich sought to elide. Yet Rich's ghazals leave a remarkable record of the late 1960s' cultural moment, as poets sought to fuse their political and formal commitments, forging alliances with fellow artist-activists.

During the last two decades gay and lesbian poets have reinvigorated the love sonnet. Yet scholarship in the field neglects this achievement because it fits uneasily between queer studies' commitment to new verse forms and many prosodists' hostility to identity politics. My third chapter seeks to rectify this oversight, showing how writers such as Rafael Campo, Marilyn Hacker, and Henri Cole discover a new relation to the form's Petrarchan past, an avenue around the impasse that the form otherwise faces.

While the sestina is rare in English-language poetry before the twentieth century and the ghazal almost nonexistent, the sonnet and the heroic couplet are mainstays of the canonical Anglo-American poetic tradition. Yet even amid a "return" to "traditional" forms, few poets write heroic couplets. My fourth chapter explores why, pointing to the division between the disciplines of creative writing and literary scholarship and the way these institutional divisions inform a very different understanding of the heroic couplet and eighteenth-century poetry and culture.

The ballad presents an opportunity for a more communal poetry and a point of contact between "experimental" and "traditional" poetics. Drawing examples from Charles Bernstein and Marilyn Nelson, I show that the ballad offers a manifold resource: the structure necessary for Bernstein to achieve a personal resonance often missing in recent avant-gardist work and the shared technique for Nelson to speak communally, not as a self in isolation. Building on the book's emphasis on the relations between allegedly antagonistic groups of poets, the final chapter develops a vocabulary to discuss the most interesting contemporary poetry. To do so, I propose we discuss "contemporaries" who "share the language," not partisans who wage "wars."

My study investigates five forms; it does not catalogue all the forms currently in use. I focus on American poets and international poets, including Derek Walcott, Seamus Heaney, and Agha Shahid Ali, whose work exerts considerable influence on the contemporary American poetry scene. By its very nature, then, my study leaves out a host of poets and forms worthy of attention; the omitted forms include, but certainly are not limited to, the villanelle, pantoum, and cento. Though regrettable, such omissions are inevitable for a study of this size and scope. More agreeably, they provide subjects for future research.

While arguing that this metrical verse remains more interesting and vital than commonly accepted, I feel little need to pit "closed" verse against "open." It is important to note the instances when a poet such as Derek Walcott employs poetic form to signal his distaste for a certain, historically specific, kind of free verse. Yet much more common are other kinds of exchanges, where poets associated with different verse traditions inspire and inform each other's work, by suggesting new avenues for exploration. In this spirit, I take my title, *Questions of Possibility*, not from a sonnet or sestina but from Lyn Hejinian's *My Life*, a work in what John Ashbery calls "the other tradition." Composed of thirty-seven prose poems of thirty-seven sentences apiece (in the first edition) then forty-five sections of forty-five sentences (in the second edition), Hejinian's book expresses the hope that inspires this study when she writes, "Any work dealing with questions of possibility must lead to new work."[31]

ONE

"THE AGE OF THE SESTINA"

IN JULY 1937, ELIZABETH BISHOP PUBLISHED HER RECENTLY COMPLETED poem, "A Miracle for Breakfast." I quote it in full:

> At six o'clock we were waiting for coffee,
> waiting for coffee and the charitable crumb
> That was going to be served from a certain balcony,
> —like kings of old, or like a miracle.
> It was still dark. One foot of the sun
> steadied itself on a long ripple in the river.
>
> The first ferry of the day had just crossed the river.
> It was so cold we hoped that the coffee
> would be very hot, seeing that the sun
> was not going to warm us; and that the crumb
> would be a loaf each, buttered, by a miracle.
> At seven a man stepped out on the balcony.
>
> He stood for a minute alone on the balcony
> looking over our heads towards the river.
> A servant handed him the makings of the miracle,
> consisting of one lone cup of coffee
> and one roll, which he proceeded to crumb,
> his head, so to speak, in the clouds—along with the sun.

Was the man crazy? What under the sun
was he trying to do, up there on his balcony!
Each man received one rather hard crumb,
which some flicked scornfully into the river
and, in a cup, one drop of the coffee.
Some of us stood around, waiting for the miracle.

I can tell what I saw next; it was not a miracle.
A beautiful villa stood in the sun
and from its doors came the smell of hot coffee.
In front, a baroque white plaster balcony
added by birds, who nest along the river,
—I saw it with one eye close to the crumb—

and galleries and marble chambers. My crumb
my mansion, made for me by a miracle,
through ages, by insects, birds, and the river
working the stone. Every day, in the sun,
at breakfast time I sit on my balcony
with my feet up, and drink gallons of coffee.

We licked up the crumb and swallowed the coffee.
A window across the river caught the sun
as if the miracle were working, on the wrong balcony.[1]

Like all sestinas, "A Miracle for Breakfast" conforms to an intricate, predetermined formula. The opening stanza introduces six endwords— "coffee," "crumb," "balcony," "miracle," "sun," and "river"—which repeat through six sestets. Starting with the second sestet, each stanza duplicates the previous stanza's endwords in the following order: last, first, fifth, second, fourth, then third. Thus, "coffee," "crumb," "balcony," "miracle," "sun," and "river" are reordered into "river," "coffee," "sun," "crumb," "miracle," and "balcony." By the poem's end, each endword appears in all six lines. Finally, according to a convention that some modern writers subvert but Bishop adheres to, the concluding envoy features two endwords in each of its three lines, one as an endword and one in the middle of the line:

We licked up the *crumb* and swallowed the *coffee*.
A window across the *river* caught the *sun*
as if the *miracle* were working, on the wrong *balcony*. (my italics)

Bishop later called "A Miracle for Breakfast" "my Depression poem": "It was written shortly after the time of the souplines and men selling apples, around 1936 or so. It was my 'social conscious' poem, a poem about hunger."[2] The quotation marks punctuate Bishop's serious reservations about "'social conscious'" literature. Remembering "the Marxist '30s," Bishop insisted she knew much more than "most of the college girls [who] didn't know much about social conditions": "I was very aware of the Depression—some of my family were much affected by it. After all, anybody who went to New York and rode the Elevated could see that things were wrong. But I had lived with poor people and knew something of poverty at firsthand" (Schwartz and Estess, *Elizabeth Bishop*, 293–94). Despite this firsthand knowledge, Bishop consistently refused to characterize herself as a political writer. "I was always opposed to political thinking as such for writers," she declared, "Politically I considered myself a socialist, but I disliked 'social conscious' writing" (ibid., 293).

Behind "A Miracle for Breakfast" stands W. H. Auden's "Hearing of harvests rotting in the valleys"; beside it one might place Louis Zukofsky's "Mantis." Written over a five-year period, from 1932 to 1937, each of these sestinas is a "Depression poem," "a poem about hunger." Auden writes about "these starving cities"; Zukofsky describes "armies of the poor" huddled in the New York subway, the scene Bishop named as unarguable proof "that things were wrong."[3] Only a few decades separated these poems from Pound's "Sestina: Altaforte," the most famous post-Renaissance attempt in the form. Needing, as its author wryly noted, "a 54 inch chest" to read aloud, Pound's "blood-curdling" celebration of when "swords clash" remained deliberately anachronistic, from its speaker to its setting and language.[4] Departing from Pound's model in theme and style, the three sestinas written in the 1930s modernized the form. Witnessing the Great Depression, they introduced modern life to this archaic structure.

Before these poems, the sestina remained an extremely minor form in English. Invented by Arnaut Daniel and made famous by Petrarch and Dante, it entered English literature during the sixteenth century. A period of less than two decades, though, witnessed the sestina's introduction into English and its virtual disappearance. Sir Philip Sidney's "Ye goatherd gods" and Barnabe Barnes's "Sestine 5," a double and a triple sestina respectively, made a single one seem beside the point. "For over two centuries," John Frederick Nims notes, the sestina "hardly lifted its voice: there is not a single sestina in the three volumes of the Oxford anthologies that cover the seventeenth, eighteenth, and nineteenth centuries."[5] Both English and Continental neoclassicism spurned the sestina: for more than a century, no poet in any language wrote in the form.[6] The sestina did enjoy a brief acceptance in the nineteenth century, as the Pre-Raphaelite poets rediscovered it. Ironically, though, the resulting vogue further trivialized the sestina: "the 19th century / Used the 'form,'" Zukofsky notes, "And our time takes count against them" (Zukofsky, *All the Collected Short Poems*, 76–77).

From the 1930s to the present, though, the sestina has enjoyed a popularity unrivaled during any other period in Anglo-American literary history.[7] During no other time have so many poets written works of such high quality in this form or close variations of it. An extremely partial list would include poems not only by Auden, Zukofsky, and Bishop, but T. S. Eliot, W. S. Merwin, John Ashbery, James Merrill, Anthony Hecht, Donald Justice, Marilyn Hacker, and Seamus Heaney.[8] Interest in the form has continued during periods dominated by free verse; even poets famously hostile to metrical verse have published sestinas.[9] In comparison, the nineteenth century, the only period that approaches the twentieth century's fascination with the sestina, produced a far narrower accomplishment. If, as in James E. B. Breslin's curt dismissal, the postwar years were "the age of the sestina," that "age" has not yet passed.[10]

A milestone in the form's development, "A Miracle for Breakfast" offers the opportunity to consider why the sestina rose from obscurity to prominence. What advantages did this exotic form offer Bishop? Why did she, like Auden and Zukofsky, find the sestina amenable to what Zukofsky called "the most pertinent subject of our day—/ The poor"?[11] What insights did the next generation glean from sestinas such as "A Miracle for Breakfast"? How have metrical writers coming of age in the 1950s, poets such as Anthony Hecht and Donald Justice, built upon their accomplishments?

As Bishop's comments suggest, both political and aesthetic pressures motivated her formal choices. The Great Depression, "the time of souplines and men selling apples," demanded her attention. Yet the situation also posed a dilemma: how could an author who categorically disliked "'social conscious' poetry" write a "social conscious" poem?

In a letter to Marianne Moore dated September 15, 1936, Bishop called the sestina "a sort of stunt."[12] This triviality recommended the form. Bishop wanted to avoid writing what she saw as a sloganeering poetry that exists to advance a political point, to show the author's "social consciousness." The sestina, a "[c]omplicated [verse form] of great technical difficulty" (as Auden called it), foregrounds the craft of verse making.[13] Regardless of its subject, the poem remains a highly stylized literary performance. Its writer must grapple with the form's rigorous difficulties, its conspicuous technical demands. By doing so, Bishop wrote her "'social conscious' poem, a poem about hunger" that differed from the usual procedures of "'social conscious' writing."

The poem's transition from its fourth and fifth stanzas illustrates this point:

> Some of us stood around, waiting for the miracle.
>
> I can tell what I saw next; it was not a miracle.
> A beautiful villa stood in the sun
> and from its doors came the smell of hot coffee.
> In front, a baroque white plaster balcony
> added by birds, who nest along the river
> —I saw it with one eye close to the crumb . . .

This passage's sudden reversal, "I can tell what I saw next; it was not a miracle," turns a hazard into an advantage. As a sestina moves from one stanza to the next, it risks bland predictability and repetitiousness because the opening line of each stanza after the first repeats the previous line's endword. Exploiting this structure, "A Miracle for Breakfast" primes its readers to expect another unqualified occurrence of "miracle." Two stanzas before, Bishop introduces "the makings of the miracle." The line before reminds readers that they, like the members of the breadline, are "waiting for the miracle." Yet the poem delivers exactly the opposite: "not a miracle." Thus, the verse form enacts an antimiraculous epiphany, a discovery of both the meaning the verse line employs and the meaning it withholds.

It would be a great understatement to say that 1930s poetic culture liked this kind of wordplay. Bishop wrote "A Miracle for Breakfast" within months of first reading William Empson's *Seven Types of Ambiguity*, the decade's most celebrated work of poetry criticism. In the opening chapter Empson rediscovers Sidney's "Ye goatherd gods," praising it for exemplifying the first type of ambiguity, which arises when "a word or grammatical structure is effective in several ways at once."[14] Sidney's sestina appeals to Empson because the form demands this prized "ambiguity"; by design, a sestina uses the same endwords differently in each stanza. Empson's argument lent significant critical authority to Bishop's strategy. If literariness meant verbal ambiguity, the sestina possessed it in abundance.

Seven Types of Ambiguity remains a crucial work in the development of the sestina because it also inspired poets by infuriating them. While Bishop found encouragement in *Seven Types of Ambiguity*, W. H. Auden read the book as a challenge. In his commentary on Auden's work, John Fuller calls Auden's "Hearing of harvests rotting in the valleys," "a conscious effort to rebut" Empson's conclusion that "the capacity to accept a limitation so unflinchingly, the capacity even to conceive so large a form as a unit of sustained feeling, is one that has been lost since that age."[15]

In the 1930s, then, a confluence of forces made the sestina attractive. Empson's celebrated rediscovery of "Ye goatherd gods" drew attention to the form. The Great Depression demanded a literary response, but the prevailing aesthetic, with its emphasis on ambiguity as an essential literary characteristic, frowned upon "'social conscious' writing." The sestina provided a strategy to balance these competing claims. Its rarity in English added another incentive. Compared to other metrical forms such as the sonnet or the heroic couplet, the sestina claimed extremely few works of quality in the language. Thus, it offered poets a hardly used form sanctioned by critical authority, a field both wide open and defended.

If "A Miracle for Breakfast" employed the sestina in order to assert a certain kind of literariness, the poem revealed more about the form than it intended. In "A Miracle for Breakfast," individuals face systematic oppression, a societal indifference to their suffering:

> The first ferry of the day had just crossed the river.
> It was so cold we hoped the coffee
> would be very hot, seeing that the sun
> was not going to warm us; and that the crumb
> would be a loaf each buttered, by a miracle.
> At seven a man stepped out on the balcony.

> He stood for a minute alone on the balcony
> looking over our heads towards the river.
> A servant handed him the makings of the miracle,
> Consisting of one lone cup of coffee
> and one roll, which he proceeded to crumb,
> His head, so to speak, in the clouds—along with the sun.

As in the rest of the poem, these stanzas present a strictly regimented schedule. The breadline forms at six o'clock, before the day's first ferry takes the employed to work. The man appears on the balcony at seven. He pauses for one minute then divides "one lone cup of coffee" and "one roll" so each person can receive exactly "one rather hard crumb" and "one drop of the coffee."

It is difficult not to hear the sestina's structure echo this cruel schedule. To borrow a phrase from Leslie Fiedler's remarkable essay on Dante's stony sestina, a certain "cold mathematics" governs both transactions.[16] Shivering outside, the poor pray for a miracle to break the day's grim routine. But just as society offers further humiliations, not relief, the sestina insists that the poem follow its harsh demands. The verse line's predictability echoes the breadline's; nothing interrupts either from their progress. Bishop's new critical training taught her that poetic form could insist upon the poem's literariness, its separation from contemporary social pressures. At the same time, her "Depression poem," her poem about systematic oppression, employs a form whose harshly arbitrary demands echo its subject's.

To reformulate this idea in more general terms, the sestina's demands are so harshly arbitrary that they ask to be used metaphorically. Ten years after finishing "Hearing of harvests rotting in the valleys," W. H. Auden gave it a title also suitable for Bishop's sestina: "Paysage Moralisé." "A Miracle for Breakfast" presents a strongly moralized Depression landscape: its most prominent features—the figures who inhabit it, the spatial relations between the man on the balcony and the people below, the cold sun, and the "rather hard crumb" each man receives—are clearly allegorical. Inflected with moral outrage, the verse form acts more subtly. It registers a bitter awareness that (as Bishop said of the Depression) "things were wrong":

We licked up the crumb and swallowed the coffee.
A window across the river caught the sun
As if the miracle were working, on the wrong balcony.

A sestina's envoy reveals the endwords' final relation. In "A Miracle for Breakfast," the six endwords culminate in a morally offensive alliance. "Crumb," "coffee," "river," "sun," "miracle," and "balcony" conspire to starve the hungry of their dignity. The "crumb" and "coffee" bring little relief, the "sun" turns into a mirage of warmth, a reflection "across the river," and the waited-for "miracle" transpires only in the imagination, in the realm of simile. Tellingly, the poem's last word not required by the verse form is "wrong."

Once modernized, the sestina quickly shed its status as a minor form, eccentric within English-language literary tradition. Yet, critical respect did not follow the form's new popularity. At the same time poets create an unparalleled achievement, the sestina suffers a general contempt, as a wide range of contemporary prosodists, literary historians, poets, and poet-critics express serious reservations about the sestina's appropriateness and range.[17] The most common complaint is that sestinas are "retrograde."[18] A recent study of contemporary poetry rather flatly states: "We might say that the sestina, like other rigid and predetermined forms, is a relic of its age, the age of determinism, the age of classical (Newtonian) physics, the age in which all knowledge of the physical world was certain knowledge, predetermined knowledge. As such it has little relevance to our age of uncertainty."[19] The shrewdest metrical writers who followed Auden and Bishop learned exactly the opposite lesson. "Depression poems" such as "A Miracle for Breakfast" and "Hearing of harvests rotting in the valleys" revealed the sestina's modernity; they proved that the form could confront the age's most urgent challenges.

They did so by establishing a series of paradoxes that characterizes the most interesting recent explorations in the form. The attitude is paradoxical because expressive contradictions mark the poems' relationship to the verse structure and cultural conditions. Bishop turns to the sestina form in order to establish a distance from contemporary social conditions; by doing so, "A Miracle for Breakfast" paradoxically establishes the archaic form's relevance. The poem's apparent resistance organizes its implicit recognition of contemporary culture's particular contours. As in much recent art, ranging from dance to architecture, the poets who follow Bishop use conspicuous rules but deny the rules' authority; they compose highly formalized works when considering cultures verging on revolution, anarchy, and barbarity.

These paradoxes find their most direct representation in an increasingly popular kind of verse. "I'm sick of these sestinas," a recent poem declares. Yet the poem itself is a sestina, wittily pursuing a well-established strategy. While other forms inspire self-justifications such as sonnets on the sonnet, modern poets write sestinas *against* the sestina. They insult it as "an exercise to build technique rather than taste," "a nightmare of blank circles," and "a ball and chain." As if trapped in a "party conversation, / Formally repetitious, wilfully dull," the poets beg for the sestina to "BE GONE ! ! !"[20]

While such sestinas against the sestina might be classified as illuminating special cases, scholarship also continues to slight the contemporary sestina's more varied achievements. A widespread distaste for postwar and contemporary metrical verse lies behind the sestina's critical neglect. Disparaged as the "rear guard" or the "academics," writers such as Anthony Hecht and Donald Justice find themselves cast rather unflatteringly, as the foils for the self-professed avant-garde.[21] Even revisionist scholarship which "makes the case that the poetics of the 'tranquillized fifties' (Robert Lowell's term) were much more conflicted and poignant than we tend to assume" disregards these poets, following previous assessments that the period's most interesting work acts as "a point of departure from the academic, from the Eliotic model of rhetoric, formalism, and iambics."[22]

A closer attention to sestinas written during the postwar and contemporary eras does more than complicate the popular story of American verse as a battle between the heroic "avant-garde" and the vanquished "rear guard." Instead, highlighting the literary-historical naïveté that undermines much scholarship in the field, sestinas such as Anthony Hecht's "The Book of Yolek" and Donald Justice's "Here in Katmandu" give a clearer sense of poets' recent accomplishments in the form.

> Hecht's "The Book of Yolek" begins with a deceptive casualness:
> The dowsed coals fume and hiss after your meal
> Of grilled brook trout, and you saunter off for a walk

Down the fern trail, it doesn't matter where to,
Just so you're weeks and worlds away from home,
And among midsummer hills have set up camp
In the deep bronze glories of declining day.

You remember, peacefully, an earlier day
In childhood, remember a quite specific meal:
A corn roast and bonfire in summer camp.
That summer you got lost on a Nature Walk;
More than you dared admit, you thought of home;
No one else knows where the mind wanders to.[23]

This passage seems to present the complacency of a cultivated intellect at play. Like the addressed figure who "saunter[s] off for a walk," the poem luxuriates in the sensuousness it details, the "meal / Of grilled brook trout" and "the deep bronze glories of declining day." The poem proceeds "peacefully" with a refined yet conversational tone. Indeed, the line, "No one else knows where the mind wanders to" might serve as a motto for postwar metaphysical verse written under Eliot's influence. Like Richard Wilbur's famous simile of the mind "like some bat" whose "graceful error may correct the cave," Hecht's handling of the sestina form registers two hallmarks of that style: the privacy of any individual's thoughts and their potentially limitless range.[24] Fulfilling this ideal, the opening stanzas flaunt the ease with which the poet navigates the sestina's daunting parameters.

The poem takes a dramatic turn in the third stanza. The mind does carelessly "wander" but finds itself driven to a particularly horrific memory. The speaker remains haunted by the luck that saved his life and by his friend who did not share his good fortune:

The fifth of August, 1942.

It was morning and very hot. It was the day
They came at dawn with rifles to The Home
For Jewish Children, cutting short the meal
Of bread and soup, lining them up to walk
In close formation off to a special camp.

How often you have thought about that camp,
As though in some strange way you were driven to,
And about the children, and how they were made to walk,

> Yolek who had bad lungs, who wasn't a day
> Over five years old, commanded to leave his meal
> And shamble between armed guards to his long home.
>
> We're approaching August again. It will drive home
> The regulation torments of that camp
> Yolek was sent to, his small, unfinished meal,
> The electric fences, the numeral tattoo,
> The quite extraordinary heat of the day
> They were forced to take that terrible walk.
>
> (Hecht, Transparent Man, 73)

In these stanzas, Hecht's handling of the sestina form turns uncanny. Consistent with Freud's classic study, "The 'Uncanny'" (1919), the poem features Yolek as the speaker's double, the return of the dead, and the "doubling, dividing and interchanging of the self."[25] More relevant than these thematic correspondences, though, "The Book of Yolek" exploits the "factor of involuntary repetition" that Freud argues plays a crucial role in the uncanny (Freud, "Uncanny," 237). According to Freud, events must be repeated in order to be uncanny; this repetition "surrounds what would otherwise be innocent enough with an uncanny atmosphere, and forces upon us the idea of something fateful and inescapable when otherwise we should have spoken only of 'chance'" (ibid., 237). The repetitions' proximity to each other intensifies their effect. In an example generated from his own experience, Freud notes that a cloakroom ticket numbered "62" would seem unthreatening. If that number, however, appeared on the ticket, a cabin door, and several other places during a single day, the viewer might interpret it as an omen of the years he is destined to live. Thus, these uncanny repetitions transform "62" into "something fateful and inescapable."

"The Book of Yolek" features "the obstinate recurrence" of particular words, not "a number" (ibid., 238). Like the first appearance of 62, the endwords start innocently. "[M]eal," "walk," "to," "home," "camp," and "day" establish a vocabulary of sustenance and comfort. Repetition, though, makes these endwords menacing. The leisurely walk turns into the "terrible walk," a forced march to a horrific death, and the bucolic "summer camp" changes into a Nazi death camp. Hecht's earlier sestina, "Sestina d'Inverno" culminates in the realization that patterns "neither to our mind nor of our making" act as "destiny."[26] In its sixth stanza "The Book of Yolek" achieves a similar, albeit more horrifying understanding:

> Whether on a silent, solitary walk
> Or among crowds, far off or safe at home,
> You will remember, helplessly, that day,
> And the smell of smoke, and the loudspeakers of the camp.
> Wherever you are, Yolek will be there, too.
> His unuttered name will interrupt your meal.
> Prepare to receive him in your home some day.
> Though they killed him in the camp they sent him to,
> He will walk in as you're sitting down to a meal.
>
> (Hecht, *Transparent Man*, 74)

The pressure that the sestina form exerts on the reader and the poet echoes the speaker's helplessness. The repetitions are "involuntary": just as the speaker can control neither the past nor Yolek's ghostly interruptions of his life, the poet must follow the endwords' prescribed pattern. The opening stanza parades a sense of freedom, as its single sentence leisurely performs the tasks that the sestina sets. In contrast, the sixth stanza features a new terseness:

> Wherever you are, Yolek will be there, too.
> His unuttered name will interrupt your meal.

Instead of triumphant ingenuity, this handling of the sestina form conveys a sense of predestined limits. The endwords' repetitions haunt the final stanzas, acting as burdens to be endured, not occasions for eloquent transcendence. In Freud's terms, they instill "the idea of something fateful and inescapable" (Freud, "Uncanny," 237).

Achieving these uncanny effects from the sestina form, "The Book of Yolek" stages a fall from innocence. In the opening stanzas, the boy lives in a prelapsarian state, "an earlier day." For him "camp" means only "summer camp," and the "walk" he takes is "a Nature Walk," another opportunity to witness earth's bounty. While the boy experiences these words as essentially new and full of possibility, the mature speaker knows too much to enjoy this luxury. The uncanny repetitions of "walk" and "camp" carry the double burden of their increasingly sinister meanings haunted by far happier previous associations. For the child, "home" remains a concept largely untraumatized by confusion; even when lost, his mind freely wanders back to it. By the end of the poem, the mature speaker and the poem itself can regard only ironically home defined as a place of protection and security. Indeed, the sixth stanza's phrase, "safe at home," carries a bitter edge: the "Home / For Jewish Children" is where Nazis round up their victims; home is where a survivor awaits his ghost.

Hecht's uncanny handling of the sestina form evokes a torment larger than the speaker's psychological distress. Hecht belongs to that generation of Jewish intellectuals who experienced the Holocaust as a crisis of Western humanism. Hecht witnessed firsthand the concentration camps' horrors, when his infantry troop helped to capture Flossenburg. The epigraph, which he characterizes as "the text of a stirring chorus of Bach's 'St. John Passion,'" introduces the bitter paradox that, in George Steiner's anguished observation, "In our own day the high places of literacy, of philosophy, of artistic expression, became the setting for Belsen. . . . Barbarism prevailed on the very ground of Christian humanism, of Renaissance culture and classic rationalism."[27] Raising this point, the epigraph quotes the "stirring chorus" that translates into German Jesus' words in John 19:7: "We have a law, and by our law he ought to die." By the Nazi's law, Yolek ought to die. Thus, a line from the New Testament revised into art rationalizes murder.

The sestina form similarly meditates upon the relationship between "Christian humanism" and "barbarism." Although, as I have noted, the sestina remains a little used form in English until the twentieth century, it dates back to the advent of Renaissance humanism and to its two most celebrated poets, Petrarch and Dante. While the opening stanzas depict childhood innocence, the form itself self-consciously belongs to the sestina's pastoral tradition.[28] The comfort with which "The Book of Yolek" proceeds through this pastoral landscape familiar to sestinas by Dante, Petrarch, Spenser, and Sidney announces Hecht's debt to them. Yet the poem's relationship to its verse form turns increasingly claustrophobic, until the sestina's impositions echo those of the Holocaust. A "law" condemns Yolek to die, while "the laws of the poetic art," the "laws that stand for other laws," "govern" the poem.[29] The fifth stanza most forcefully raises this point. Tellingly, the "torments" Yolek suffers are called "regulation" and the concentration camp "tattoos" "numeral tattoos," suggestive of the mathematical progressions, the "regulation torments," that control the sestina form.

Indeed, the sestina's repetitions evoke a particularly grim view of history. Recognizing the forceful reality of violence in twentieth-century life, Hecht seizes upon the sestina form's strong sense of predetermination in order to depict history as a cycle of genocide and tortured remembrance. Like all sestinas, "The Book of Yolek" meditates upon a set of six endwords. These endwords remain the same while their meanings shift. In the process, the sestina form remakes homey rituals of daily life, a "meal," a "walk," a "day," into violence-scarred moments. The envoy exemplifies this movement:

> Prepare to receive him in your home some day.
> Though they killed him in the camp they sent him to,
> He will walk in as you're sitting down to a meal.

What's striking about this stanza is how much of its information is, literally speaking, repetitious. An attentive reader already realizes that the Nazis killed Yolek, a Jewish boy with "bad lungs" taken to a concentration camp. Similarly, the rest of the envoy conveys information already established in the previous stanza, especially its declaration that

> Wherever you are, Yolek will be there, too.
> His unuttered name will interrupt your meal.

Yet Hecht rightly does not omit the envoy in favor of a more economical conclusion. Instead, "The Book of Yolek" stresses that violence haunts this century as predictably as the envoy ends the sestina.

In the poem's own terms, "The Book of Yolek" "drive[s] home" the difference between appreciating a fact as horrible as the Holocaust and knowing it. Robert Jay Lifton and Eric Markusen have noted how, during the Holocaust, many Jews "could simultaneously believe and not believe that the Nazis were murdering very large numbers of fellow Jews":

> This "dual belief" has been called "middle knowledge" in relation
> to dying patients. . . . Characteristic of this duality is that one has

an active psychological inclination toward each side of contradictory beliefs; thus, in the midst of Auschwitz, some people could not quite take in the truth of the gas chambers. And later, a Jewish physician-survivor told how, after about two years in Auschwitz and almost forty years of working medically with survivors, "I still cannot believe that they did it . . . That anyone would try to round up all the Jews in Europe to kill them."[30]

Though any artistic rendering categorically differs from the experience of genocide, Hecht's handling of the sestina form arouses a "dual belief" akin to what Lifton and Markusen describe. In particular, "The Book of Yolek" plays off the fact that a child's death is too terrible to await, to know that it will occur, without also believing that it will not. Once line 18 turns "camp" into Nazi death camp, the reader understands that meaning is too forceful not to return. Each subsequent repetition of "camp" confirms this belief that Yolek will die. Yet every repetition of "camp" also raises the hope that the word might return to its more bucolic opening meaning, where "midsummer hills have set up camp / In the deep bronze glories of declining day." The sestina encourages this hope by waiting until its second-to-last line to concede Yolek's death. By prolonging its acknowledgment of Yolek's murder, the poem urges the reader to adopt two contradictory positions, to anticipate Yolek's death and to anticipate his equally unimaginable survival. For this reason, the envoy's full acknowledgment of Yolek's murder is both startling and wholly predictable.

Finally, "The Book of Yolek" addresses the much-debated question of "poetry after Auschwitz."[31] In a 1992 lecture, Hecht celebrates "the contrariety of impulses" that he claims defines the greatest works of art:

> I have attempted here to make the claim that the richest, most eloquent and durable of the arts in general, and poetry in particular, is always multivalenced, and implicitly when not explicitly dialectical. And this dialectical, self-critical discordance performs two functions simultaneously. It allows the poet to achieve a certain healthy impersonality, serving as a device by which to inhibit any limp tendency to narcissistic solipsism, on the one hand; on the other, it lends to the poetry itself the rich complexity of actuality—the unsimplified plentitude of the objective world. (Hecht, On the Laws, 130)

Consistent with these principles, many of Hecht's most successful poems employ elegant, almost fussily elaborate language and metrical forms when describing, in great detail, base subjects such as the specific methods torturers and mass murderers favor. Hecht's strategy sets a dialectic between a high style uncommon in contemporary poetry and the atrocities too common in life, between the formal pleasures of art and the expert infliction of misery.

"The Book of Yolek" works similarly. The sestina's structure acknowledges "the rich complexity of actuality," an order beyond the individual's control. Hecht's handling of the form celebrates the cultures that produced the sestina and its previous masters; without Dante and Petrarch and, more immediately, Auden, Bishop, and Empson, "The Book of Yolek" could not have been written. The poem also honors metrical skill, the graceful handling of difficult poetic forms, as an artistic and cultural virtue, the demonstration of civilized learning and technical dexterity. As soon as Hecht's poetry, like his prose, gestures with "one hand," it raises "the other." To understand "the rich complexity of actuality," poetic form must be "dialectical" and "self-critical," acknowledging not only the world's goodness but its evil. The form that allows the poet to demonstrate freedom within strict limits also inspires a claustrophobic sense of confinement. By implication and association, it entertains the culpability of the culture and the values it celebrates. Indeed, as I have noted, the sestina's intricate organizations echo the camp's "regulation torments."

The poem's handling of its endwords most clearly expresses this idea. Hecht, unlike Bishop, allows himself the flexibility to substitute homonyms for the original endword: "to," for example, changes into "1942," "tattoo," and "too." These homonyms might be called traditional, as many precedents for them exist in the sestina's long history. Dante, for example, substituted the Italian words for "necks," "seizes," and "hills," all of which are homonyms. In a more celebrated gesture, Petrarch interchanged the words for "laurel tree" and "gold," "Laura" and "the breeze."[32] Homonyms such as "1942" and "tattoo" show this kind of verbal deftness; they acknowledge both the literary tradition that makes this technique possible and their language's richness. They also display wit by bringing together two disparate entities: a date and an indelible mark of the flesh. Yet verbal deftness, wit, and a deference to literary tradition seem desperately insufficient techniques to come to terms with the Holocaust. The words "1942" and "tattoo" risk bad taste by forming a rhyme more common to comic poetry.

In order to appreciate Hecht's approach, it might be helpful to compare it to another poet's method when writing about a similarly horrific event. In a 1985 interview, Rita Dove describes the process of composing her widely anthologized poem "Parsley," which considers the murder of 20,000 Black Haitians. As Dove recounts, Trujillo, the Dominican dictator, separated those who would live from those who would be slaughtered by the ability to roll the letter "r" in *perejil*, the Spanish word for "parsley":

> That poem took a long time to write! I started with the facts and that in a certain way almost inhibited me: the very action, the fact that he thought up this word, was already so amazing that I had a hard time trying to figure out how to deal with it. So when I wrote the poem I tried it in many different ways. I tried a sestina, particularly in the second part, "The Palace," simply because the obsessiveness of the sestina, the repeated words, was something I wanted to get—that driven quality—in the poem. I gave up the sestina very early. It was too playful for the poem. A lot of the words stayed—the key words like *parrot* and *spring* and, of course, *parsley*"[33]

Explicating this passage, Helen Vendler neatly summarizes the artistic values that inspire Dove's revisions, praising what she calls Dove's "principled refusal" of the sestina form because "such 'playfulness' threatens to interfere with a more important part of the poem's 'fit,' its moral seriousness."[34] Accordingly, Dove abandons the sestina form because "[i]t was too playful" for a subject as grim as mass murder, a point that "The Book of Yolek" certainly contests. More significantly, Dove, like Vendler, believes that a poem's form should match its subject, correspond to it fairly directly. A "playful" subject demands a "playful" form; a "serious" subject, a "serious" form. To revise Hecht's phrase, both Dove and Vendler seek a similarity of impulses.

For Hecht, the most appalling subjects often demand the most complicated forms. The reason is paradoxical: Hecht's formal elegance works best when considering events that make it seem almost beside the point. It is impossible to write about the Holocaust without some feelings of ambivalence, some questions about the appropriateness of creating art out of such suffering. Because the poetry Hecht admires

"is always multivalenced, and implicitly if not explicitly dialectical,"
the sestina, an intricate form routinely dismissed as too slight to bear
history's pressures, invites him to stage "the rich complexity of actuality."
What Steiner calls "humanism" and "barbarity" coexist in Hecht's
poetry as they do in the world. The sestina's "playful" structure mimics
the century's most fearful rhythms; the form that helped Dante to praise
his mistress's unattainable beauty confronts the Holocaust's ugliness. It
is wholly appropriate, then, that the poem's cleverest manipulations of
the sestina form occur during the poem's most awful moments: when
the endword "home" becomes "The Home / For Jewish Children" and
"to" transforms into a concentration camp "tattoo."

While Hecht employs the sestina form as a searching vehicle for
historical inquiry, Donald Justice's "Here in Katmandu" depicts the
sestina as nearly exhausted, burdened with diminished possibilities.
Published in *Summer Anniversaries*, which won the 1959 Lamont
award, the poem is one of Justice's "fashionably sad" "early poems."[35]
Considering Edmund Hillary's and Tenzing Norgay's recent ascent of
Everest, it less celebrates the triumph than laments the deflation after
their return:

> We have climbed the mountain,
> There's nothing more to do.
> It is terrible to come down
> To the valley
> Where, amidst many flowers,
> One thinks of snow,
>
> As, formerly, amidst snow,
> Climbing the mountain,
> One thought of flowers,
> Tremulous, ruddy with dew,
> In the valley.
> One caught their scent coming down.
>
> It is difficult to adjust, once down,
> To the absence of snow.
> Clear days, from the valley,
> One looks up at the mountain.
> What else is there to do?
> Prayerwheels, flowers!

Let the flowers
Fade, the prayerwheels run down.
What have these to do
With us who have stood atop the snow
Atop the mountain,
Flags seen from the valley?

It might be possible to live in the valley,
To bury oneself among flowers,
If one could forget the mountain,
How, setting out before dawn,
Blinded with snow,
One knew what to do.

Meanwhile it is not easy here in Katmandu,
Especially when to the valley
That wind which means snow
Elsewhere, but here means flowers,
Comes down,
As soon it must, from the mountain.[36]

Justice wrote "Here in Katmandu" after watching "The Conquest of Everest," the BBC's award-winning documentary where the poet (as he later remembered) "got my information."[37] The film opens with a military band's procession. Crowds cheer and wave handkerchiefs, not to celebrate Everest's ascent but to hail Queen Elizabeth II, as her gilded chariot passes, returning her from the coronation. The voiceover explains: "June the second, 1953. People in London were excited, and with good reason. A queen had been crowned. On June the second everything was new and exciting. And to add to the cheers the newspapers gave an extra of extras. Britain had won a new victory! Men had climbed Mount Everest!"[38] To illustrate this point, a shot lingers on a table of quickly selling newspapers. Like the film itself, the punning headlines celebrate the coincidence of two historical events: the coronation and the ascent. "The Crowning Glory Everest Is Climbed," one proclaims, while another similarly reports, "The Crowning Glory Everest Conquered." Sharing the same cliché, the headlines insist that both milestones "crown" Britain with "glory."

The film proceeds from London to Katmandu, eliding the two celebrations: "A procession in London, another in central Asia. With garlands around their necks, the climbers come down from the top of the world. At the eleventh attempt, after thirty years of defeats, men have achieved the impossible." The film's transition is awkward because it attempts a hopeless task: to present the Everest ascent as a universally celebrated British achievement. Instead, the climbers descended to intensely political debates about which climber reached the summit first and which country, Nepal, India, or Tibet, was Tenzing's "home." These widely reported controversies engulfed both men. Tenzing needed police protection after partisans attempted to bribe and threaten him, wanting him to claim the status of "the first man on Everest." Hillary received chilly receptions from Katmandu crowds far less hospitable than those the movie presents. "Everyone in that vast crowd was pouring out hate towards me," he later remembered, "because they feared I might not be happy to remain 'the second man on Everest.' . . . At each large town the welcome was repeated and so was the reaction."[39]

"Here in Katmandu" slyly revises the imperialist ideology that the Everest expedition inspired. Shot while the British Empire slouched toward obsolescence, "The Conquest of Everest" trumpets the empire's vitality, complete with a recent present when "everything was new and exciting." The film presents a symbolic triumph for an empire more recently accustomed to defeats: a "conquest," "a new victory," another "good reason" to cheer. Though Hillary later expressed disdain for such myth making, his personality contributed to its wide acceptance in the West. A laconic New Zealander, he projected an air of masculine self-determination, a bootstrapping explorer spirit. Like the movie that lionized him, his writings, speeches, and continued explorations affirmed, "yes, there is plenty left to do" (Hillary, *Nothing Venture*, 308).

In contrast, "Here in Katmandu" depicts a postcolonial malaise. The potential for heroic accomplishment no longer exists; the present may even lack the psychic resources to imagine what a future project might be. "We have climbed the mountain, / There's nothing more to do," the poem bemoans.

This complaint echoes Justice's own reservations about the sestina form. In an interview Justice explained his dilemma, asking, "Once you've written a sestina, why write another, unless you can find something new in the form to work out?" The answer Justice discovered was the idea of a "free-verse sestina" (Justice, *Platonic Scripts*, 17, 31). Referring to his earlier, more metrically regular sestinas, he comments:

> When I was writing those sestinas, I think practically all the sestinas
> that had been written in English before, the ones I had read anyway,
> were in iambic pentameter—or at least in what I would call a casual
> pentameter, one in which the line might get longer or a little shorter,
> as in Pound's or the two by Kees. But I consciously shortened the lines;
> I varied the length of the lines. Nowadays anybody may do that. The
> Katmandu sestina has a small place in the history of the form, I think.
> (Ibid., 105)

While Justice modestly claims a "small place in the history of the
form," others view far more darkly "the free-verse sestinas" that follow
his poem. In his anthology *The Direction of Poetry: An Anthology of
Rhymed and Metered Verse Written in the English Language Since 1975*
(1988), Robert Richman cites sestinas written in metrically irregular
lines as proof and product of versification's current degradations: "The
free verse orthodoxy that has reigned for the last twenty-five years in
the United States and Great Britain has insinuated itself so deeply into
our respective poetic cultures that the entire conception of form has
been corrupted. The last two decades have seen a plethora of free verse
'sestinas.'"[40] Richman condemns Philip Dacey and David Jauss's *Strong
Measures: Contemporary American Poetry in Traditional Forms* (1986),
which includes "Here in Katmandu." *Strong Measures* is "a showcase
for precisely this kind of hybrid verse, in which the pretense of a
traditional form is used without employing any of its technical attributes"
(Richman, *Direction of Poetry*, xvi). Richman's disdain extends even to
his punctuation: note the dismissive quotation marks he places around
"sestinas" in the phrase "free verse 'sestinas.'" As these quotation marks
indicate, Richman finds such works to be offensively pretentious. In
short, he would agree with Richard Wilbur that "writing non-metrical
sestinas" "is about as bad as you can get."[41]

A free-verse sestina, then, is too "experimental" for traditionalists
and too "traditional" for those who dislike all metrical verse. In
Richman's terms, this "hybrid verse" offends the sensibilities of those
who do not want "the entire conception of form" to be "corrupted." At
the same time, other readers consider even a free verse sestina to be a
"relic" because it imposes a predetermined pattern upon the process of
composition (Stitt, *Uncertainty and Plenitude*, 31).

In the face of such hostility and obvious counterarguments, Justice's
"free-verse sestina" registers a commitment to formally innovative

metrical verse, a category that many would find oxymoronic. Introducing a new measure into the sestina form, "Here in Katmandu" couples a sense of innovation with a mindfulness of the form's past. The fifth stanza illustrates this point:

> It might be possible to live in the valley,
> To bury oneself among flowers,
> If one could forget the mountain,
> How, setting out before dawn,
> Blinded with snow,
> One knew what to do.

Consistent with the poem's acute sense of lateness, Justice conspicuously borrows from Auden's and Sidney's earlier sestinas. A formal gesture signals this relationship: Justice appropriates the endwords "valleys" and "mountains" from Auden's "Hearing of harvests rotting in the valleys" and Auden's influence, Sidney's "Ye goatherd gods." Every third line, the poet reminds himself and his readers of their precursors. By doing so, the poem introduces a literary belatedness akin to the explorer's. The poet and explorer share a similar fate, doomed to a paltry future. In a pun that the poem exploits, both have come "down" physically and emotionally.

Indeed, this languid one-sentence stanza almost seems mired in the depression it expresses. As in Pound's description of the sestina as "a form like a thin sheet of flame folding and infolding upon itself,"[42] it retreads the same basic complaint: the speaker's inability to conceive of "what to do." Like the rest of the poem, the stanza literally goes nowhere; it begins and ends in the Katmandu valley. At the same time it laments the imagination's failures, the poem traverses a great distance. It ascends, starting in the valley then descending even lower "[t]o bury oneself among flowers," before memory returns the speaker to the mountain top.

Forecasting a grimly predictable future, the poem revitalizes the form by adding a new variable. If Justice's description of his composition process can be trusted, the stanza presents a microcosm of his composition method. It starts with a line of iambic pentameter, "It might be possible to live in the valley." Subsequent lines vary this meter and shorten its length. As in the rest of the poem, the most common structure is a three-stress line, the meter that the next two lines employ:

> To bury oneself among flowers,
> If one could forget the mountain.

At least once a stanza, a dramatically shorter line such as "Blinded with snow" conspicuously departs from this pattern.

Because the poem's lines range from twelve to two syllables and from six stresses to a single one, qualitative judgments, not quantitative principles, govern their structure. Faced with a passage of metrically regular lines, even a reader untutored in versification develops a strong intuition about when the next line will stop. Justice's free-verse sestina introduces a variable to the sestina's pattern. Like the two endwords the poem borrows, its irregular meter acts as shifting point of departure. Any anticipation of when a line will, or should, end must be provisional and imprecise, closer to a guess than a confident prediction. This dynamic adds a new level of formal unpredictability to a poem that grimly bemoans the future's lack of surprise.

Justice once said of John Cage, "You know, he's the Enemy." But when the two poets met as visiting professors at the University of Cincinnati, they quickly developed a "working friendship."[43] Justice later described how Cage's example inspired him to try his own versions of chance-based composition methods. This revealing statement is worth quoting at length:

> As I recall, I got started not long after playing poker one night in Cincinnati with John Cage. Only *I* wanted to control chance, not submit to it. Chance has no taste. What I did was to make a card game out of the process of writing. I'd always loved card games anyhow, gambling in general. As well as I can recall now what I did, I made up three large decks of "vocabulary" cards—one deck each for nouns, verbs, and adjectives—and a smaller fourth deck of "syntax" cards, sentence forms with part-of-speech blanks to be filled in. I would then shuffle and deal out a sequence of "syntax" cards, then shuffle the "vocabulary" cards in their turn and fill the syntactical blanks in. I would go through all this three times, allowing myself to go back and forth as I wished across the table of results, mixing them up to taste. It sounds silly enough, I suppose, and of course anyone could do it.

But it seemed at the time to simulate, at least a little, the way the mind worked in writing.[44]

More interesting than Justice's defensive qualifications are the sympathies he discovers. Cage's method attracted him because "it seemed at the time to simulate, at least a little, the way the mind worked in writing." "How?" one might ask. Decks of vocabulary and syntax cards literalize the metaphor of poetry as a game, a metaphor Justice finds compelling. By employing "ingenious and elaborate forms" (Justice's term) or "chance operations" (Cage's), a poet wagers that arbitrary, complex constraints yield greater freedoms, that restrictions liberate.[45] Faced with otherwise eccentric formulas, the poet focuses his attention on a series of local problems; "the mind" at work resembles the shuffle of cards labeled "syntax" and "vocabulary." In this manner the poet seeks "to free oneself from one's habitual way of doing things, one's stock responses to word and sentence formation."[46] Descended from different genealogies of influence, Cage and Justice arrive at complementary positions.

One reason that Justice found himself warming to the "Enemy" was that he was already practicing some of its methods, albeit unwittingly. As Marjorie Perloff notes, Cage's poetry "slyly sneaks poetic conventions in by the back door" (Perloff, *Dance of the Intellect*, 206). "Here in Katmandu" employs this strategy in reverse: it slyly sneaks in what one might call "experimental conventions." Blurring "free" and "metrical" verse, Justice's pared-down sestina makes a "card game out of the process of writing." Each stanza shuffles the endwords, redealing "Down," "snow," "valley," "mountain," "do," and "flowers" as "flowers," "down," "do," "snow," "mountain," and "valley." The poet's role is to fill in the blanks and keep the game going.

It would be an overstatement to claim that Cage and Justice share the same aesthetic. Justice's desire "to control chance, not submit to it" differs from Cage's fuller commitment to what he called his "exploration of nonintention."[47] Yet "Here in Katmandu" craftily advances the traditions it only partially honors. It considers the period after a great achievement, when the prospects for groundbreaking work seem diminished. The poet and the explorer share this unhappy fate. The poem's formal innovations, though, relieve its unrelenting sense of belatedness, finding "something new in the form to work out" (Justice, *Platonic Scripts*, 17). It also allows the poem to negotiate the two extremes of Hillary's imperial assertiveness and its own passivity, to disprove the myth that "The Conquest of Everest" promotes and its own glum declaration, "There's nothing more to do." Writing after Sidney and Auden, and amid his contemporaries' wide accomplishments in the form, Justice does not pretend that the sestina presents a new challenge to "conquer." Instead, it pursues one of the paradoxes that Cage declared musical compositions must take: "a purposeful purposelessness" (Cage, *Silence*, 12).

TWO

"IN THAT THICKET OF
BITTER ROOTS": THE GHAZAL
IN AMERICA

IN 1968 THE GHAZAL ENTERED AMERICAN POETRY. THE YEAR 1969 MARKED
the centennial anniversary of the death of Mirza Ghalib, a Persian
and Urdu poet and one of the form's masters. In anticipation of the
anniversary, Aijaz Ahmad, a Pakistani literary and cultural critic living
in New York, solicited several well-known American poets to work on a
pamphlet of translations for the centennial. Because none of the poets
knew Urdu, the text's original language, Ahmad supplied them with
literal translations from which they crafted their collaborative versions.
Ahmad's queries generated much more enthusiasm than he anticipated.
His project expanded from a pamphlet into a handsome 174-page book,
Ghazals of Ghalib, published by Columbia University Press. Several of
the translations also appeared in major American and Indian literary
periodicals. The book's contributors included four future Pulitzer-Prize
winners who already enjoyed a certain stature in the literary community:
W. S. Merwin, Adrienne Rich, William Stafford, and Mark Strand.[1]

Moving from translation to original composition, Rich started
"Ghazals (Homage to Ghalib)" in July 1968, only a few months after
Martin Luther King's assassination and less than thirty days after Robert
Kennedy's death. Inspired by what the historian James T. Patterson calls
"the most turbulent year in the postwar history of the United States,"
she finished the ghazal sequence "The Blue Ghazals."[2] The first ghazals
published by an American writer, Rich's sequences offer the occasion to

consider how a verse form moves from one literary tradition to another: why it attracts poets and how its conventions change in order to address new literary and cultural challenges.

Of course the most familiar terms to describe Western appropriations of Eastern literary and cultural forms are "exoticism" and "orientalism." Though American ignorance and presumptiveness certainly contributed to the ghazal's sudden popularity, they do not comprise the entire story or even its most compelling part. Rich's cagey, anguished poems searchingly investigate America's difficult racial politics, seeking to forge a cross-cultural poetry of witness, a poetry of reconciliation and cross-racial identification. Her poems and the ghazals that follow them highlight the intricate, tenuous, and, at times, intense relationship between "politics" in its most common meaning and poetic form. The verse form both expresses the poet's political loyalties and complicates them, adding new resonance and unforeseen entanglements. By doing so, the ghazals suggest the difficulties that arise when poets seek to translate their political commitments into their handling of verse form.

Given American literary culture's general hostility to metrical technique, the ghazal presented an unlikely form to attract interest. Established at least one full century before the sonnet, the ghazal's structure might be called archaic, elaborate, and unyielding. Andrew McCord's translation of Ghalib's "Ghazal" demonstrates some of the form's many prescriptions. The poem begins:

> Should you not look after me another day?
> Why did you go alone? I leave in only another day.
>
> If your gravestone is not erased first my head will be.
> Genuflecting at your door, in any case, it's me another day.

As this passage illustrates, the ghazal's endstopped couplets share a strict monorhyme. Its first couplet uses only one endword or end phrase (in this case, "day"). Every subsequent couplet's final line repeats at its end that word or phrase, called the "radif." In addition, the ghazal features an internal rhyme placed immediately before the "radif," called the "qafia." This translation uses "me," which rhymes with "only" and "me." Finally, the writer mentions his or her name or pseudonym in the final couplet. Thus, the translation concludes:

> Only a fool asks me, "Ghalib why are you alive?"
> My fate is to long for the day I will not be another day.[3]

Rich's ghazals, like her translations, adhere to none of the conventions I just outlined.[4] They do, however, keep the ghazal's traditional argumentative structure, what the translator K. C. Kanda calls "the fragmentary thought-structure of the *ghazal*." "The different couplets of the *ghazal*," Kanda explains, "are not bound by the unity and consistency of thought. Each couplet is a self-sufficient unit, detachable and quotable, generally containing the complete expression of an idea."[5] In an interview Rich invokes this idea, explaining how Ghalib's ghazals provided techniques for expressing the particular "fragmentation" and "confusion" she experienced at the time:

> I certainly had to find an equivalent for the kinds of fragmentation I was feeling, and confusion. One thing that was very helpful to me was working on the translations from the Urdu poet Mirza Ghalib, which led me to write original *ghazals*. There, I found a structure which allowed for a highly associative field of images. And once I saw how that worked, I felt instinctively, this is exactly what I need, there is no traditional Western order that I have found that will contain all these materials. (Rich, *Collected Early Poems*, 426)

These comments expand Rich's note on her ghazals: "My *ghazals* are personal and public, American and twentieth-century; but they owe much to the presence of Ghalib in my mind: a poet self-educated and profoundly learned, who owned no property and borrowed his books, writing in an age of political and cultural break-up" (Rich, *Collected Early Poems*, 426).

As these telling comments suggest, two affinities drew Rich to the ghazal. First, it offered the qualities that her poetry already embraced. Like many other American poets in the late 1960s, Rich developed a disjunctive, elliptical poetics, renouncing what she called her early work's "perfection of order" in which "control, technical mastery and intellectual clarity were the real goals."[6] Though put to compelling uses, this idea was rather ordinary; a great number of American poets of Rich's generation expressed similar determinations. By doing so, Rich translated the time's sociopolitical and literary-historical contours into stylistic and formal terms. The intensification of the Vietnam War, the challenges offered by feminism and the civil rights movements, and New Criticism's waning influence all informed her decision to employ the more associative, fragmentary mode that constituted the period's major poetic style. Thus, the ghazal offered "an equivalent" both to the experience of contemporary American history and to the verse techniques that American poets favored.

Second, the ghazal's origin from outside the "West" also recommended the form to Rich. Though she described her ghazals as "American and twentieth-century," she saw the form as possessing a "structure" significantly different from any "traditional Western order," a counterlogic to Western rationalism. Of course Rich did not associate the ghazal with what one might call a "traditional Eastern order" such as the Mughal Court, where Ghalib, the royal poet, "corrected" apprentices' efforts.[7] Instead, the highly structured form expresses "fragmentation" and "confusion," not aristocratic hierarchies. Her similarly partial reading of Ghalib's biography deepened what she saw as the form's anti-imperialist resonance. In her brief portrait, Ghalib's life parallels her own, as each poet writes in "an age of political and cultural break-up." "Thousands of my friends are dead," Ghalib lamented after the Indian revolt of 1857, fought around his home in Delhi. "If I live, there is none to share my sorrow, and if I die there will be none to mourn me" (Russell and Islam, *Ghalib*, 161). The ghazal form acts as a gesture of affinity, likening Ghalib's desperation to the turmoil Rich experienced in 1968, amid the year's riots, assassinations, and war. To do so, it elides the significant differences that separate the two poets and recasts Ghalib as a rather ethereal "presence" in Rich's "mind."

In Rich's most interesting ghazals, her efforts to construct a cross-cultural poetry of witness confront this strategy's painful limits, its thwarted hopes arising from the age's troubled contradictions. In these poems, a more contemporary, more threatening "presence" also haunts the poet. Two of her ghazals address Amiri Baraka, or as Rich somewhat anachronistically calls him, LeRoi Jones, a figure whose life and art mark the boundaries of her liberal poetics. The twelfth poem in "Ghazals (Homage to Ghalib)" is the less anguished of the two:

> A dead mosquito, flattened against a door;
> his image could survive our comings and our goings.

LeRoi! Eldridge! listen to us, we are ghosts
condemned to haunt the cities where you want to be at home.

The white children turn black on the negative.
The summer clouds blacken inside the camera-skull.

Every mistake that can be made, we are prepared to make;
anything less would fall short of the reality we're dreaming.

Someone has always been desperate, now it's our turn—
we who were free to weep for Othello and laugh at Caliban.

I have learned to smell a *conservateur* a mile away:
they carry illustrated catalogues of all that there is to lose.
(Rich, *Collected Early Poems*, 350)

Written in July 1968, amid the legal wrangling that soon convinced
Eldridge Cleaver to flee to Cuba and Algiers, the poem presciently
casts Cleaver as an exile-in-the-making. Strikingly, the ghazal depicts
"LeRoi" as equally unavailable in "the cities where you want to be at
home" or, more precisely, where the speaker wants him to want to be
at home. "Someone has always been desperate, now it's our turn," the
poem insists, as whites experience an urban "desperation" previously
limited to blacks and other racial minorities. Rich's "fragmentary
thought-structure" leaves unspecified the exact causes for this white
guilt. Following her reading of the ghazal tradition, the poem is more
suggestive than declarative; it evokes a certain mood felt in American
cities during the aftermath of King's assassination and the riots that
ensued. Yet the poem fears violence less than its own inconsequence.
The insistent apostrophe, "LeRoi! Eldridge! listen to us," admits that
these leading figures in the Black Panther Party and the Black Arts
movement do not care about what Rich wants to tell them.

A poem in Rich's second ghazal sequence, "The Blue Ghazals,"
returns to Baraka and the cultural and artistic contradictions he
embodies. Dated two months later and bearing the dedication "For
LeRoi Jones," the poem recounts the disturbing experience of reading
the work of this poet who, despite the dedication, no longer called
himself "LeRoi Jones":

Late at night I went walking through your difficult wood,
half-sleepy, half-alert in that thicket of bitter roots.

Who doesn't speak to me, who speaks to me more and more,
but from a face turned off, turned away, a light shut out.

Most of the old lecturers are inaudible or dead.
Prince of the night there are explosions in the hall.

The blackboard scribbled over with dead languages
is falling and killing our children.

Terribly far away I saw your mouth in the wild light:
It seemed to me you were shouting instructions to us all.
(Rich, *Collected Early Poems*, 370)

Addressed to "a face turned off, turned away, a light shut out," this ghazal reverses the opening of one of Baraka's best-known poems, "I Substitute for the Dead Lecturer": "They have turned, and say that I am dying."[8] As Rich's lines sadly acknowledge, especially in his more recent work Baraka forcefully turned from white readers such as herself, regardless of their seemingly radical political commitments. Rich, a white, Jewish, lesbian feminist, could not help but find "difficult" and "bitter" these famously misogynistic and anti-Semitic lines from the poem that gave the Black Arts movement its name:

Look at the Liberal
Spokesman for the jews clutch his throat
. . . .
& puke himself into eternity . . . rrrrrrrr
. . . Another bad poem cracking
steel knuckles in a jewlady's mouth[9]

or these lines from *The Dead Lecturer*, which Cleaver claimed he "lived":

Rape the white girls. Rape
their fathers. Cut the mothers' throats
Black dada nihilismus, choke my friends . . . [10]

"[I]t seemed to me you were shouting instructions to us all," Rich hopefully writes. Baraka, though, stands as a stark, irrefutable assertion of difference. In his own work, he implores "Black People," not "friends" such as Rich, to "Speak This Poem / . . . LOUD" (Baraka, *Black Magic*, 117). Ironically, the more he turns from Rich, the more his "presence" haunts her. Baraka "doesn't speak to me, who speaks to me more and more," Rich writes, implying that Baraka's refusal to address a white readership only inspires a more intense engagement, a richer and more searching dialogue.

The ghazal form helps Rich to maneuver within this "thicket of bitter roots," the "difficult woods" where less oblique claims of solidarity tempt furious reassertions of difference. The form establishes what I will call a "triangulation of otherness." Rich wants poetic form to present an "equivalent" to the time's disorders. The ghazal complicates this task and makes it possible. Rich uses the ghazal to approach Baraka indirectly, invoking the authority of a poet and a form outside what she considers "traditional Western order." The verse form claims a connection with Ghalib, the putative object of veneration, in order to shorten Rich's distance to Baraka, the two poems' obsession. Employing a cagey, furtive strategy, they address Baraka through Ghalib.

Rich's verse form, then, seeks to accomplish two seemingly irreconcilable tasks. First, it attempts to reposition Rich in an international context, alleviating the nearly murderous hostility that the Black Nationalist Movement directs to her as a white, lesbian Jew. In this respect, she uses the ghazal to mitigate the more immediate pressures of contemporary American literary and political culture. She employs it as a motif, a non-Western gesture, not a prosody whose requirements she must fulfill. At the same time, Rich wants the verse form to record the very pressures that assault her. Jumping between threatening images, the ghazal's fragmentary argumentative structure evokes the age's skittish anxieties.

The next ghazal sequence written by an American poet brings into relief Rich's basic strategy. A slighter work than Rich's sequences and governed by a very different sexual politics, Jim Harrison's *Outlyer and Ghazals* (1971) also employs this "triangulation of otherness." Like Rich, Harrison uses what his author's note calls this "antique form" in order to express "whatever aspect of our life now that seemed to want to enter my field of vision."[11] In a ghazal that precedes the sequence, the speaker calls himself "[a]n enemy of civilization." Extending this motif, ghazal xxiv fantasizes about a rebellious death:

> If I were to be murdered here as an Enemy of the State you would
> have to bury me under that woodpile for want of a shovel.
>
> (Harrison, *Outlyer and Ghazals*, 21, 40)

As in Rich's poems, the ghazal form marks the speaker as somehow outside what she calls "traditional Western order." Yet the sequence shows this potential "Enemy of the State" to pale, literally and figuratively, in comparison to the real "enemy of civilization": Eldridge Cleaver and the Black Power movement he represents:

> At the post office I was given the official FBI
> Eldridge Cleaver poster—"guess he ain't around here."
>
> (Ibid., 52)

Drawing on an old racial myth, this Black Power the poem presents asserts a political and a sexual strength; in both respects, the white speaker fails to measure up:

> How could she cheat on me with that African? Let's refer
> back to the lore of the locker room & shabby albino secrets.
>
> O the shame of another's wife especially a friend's.
> Even a peek is criminal. That greener grass is brown.
>
> (Ibid., 46)

This ghazal reworks familiar myths about black male sexuality. As the speaker admits, he remains as tamely "criminal" as "a peek," especially when compared to the much more threatening and sexualized revolutionary. "I'll never be a cocksman," ghazal xxxvii meekly discloses, an inadequacy that the next poem translates this confession into political terms, "I'm not going to shoot anybody / for any revolution" (ibid., 47–48). Amid these otherwise unremarkable disclosures, the poem presents the ghazal as a similarly half-hearted rebellion, a hedge akin to the speaker's sexual and political postures. While Rich's ghazals move her closer to Baraka, a fellow poet-activist, Harrison's poems belittle their own claims of rebellious criminality.

Harrison's self-critique highlights the oddity of Rich's strategic indirection. If Baraka, not Ghalib, is Rich's true subject, why pick a form he never uses? Why not instead employ the blues form that deeply influenced Baraka's poetry? Why write ghazals to the author of *Blues People?*

In a remarkable essay, "The Blues as Poetry," Hayden Carruth, the poet, former editor of *Poetry* magazine, and the friend to whom Rich dedicated *Leaflets*, turns this set of questions into a larger complaint about American poetry and literary culture. Carruth's subject is the blues form, the three-line stanza in which the second line "worries" the first, repeating it with slight variations, and the third line rhymes with the first two.[12] Ma Rainey's "Countin' the Blues" offers a vivid example:

> Layin' in my bed with my face turned to the wall
> Lord, layin' in the bed with my face turned to the wall
> Tryin' to count these blues, so I could sing them all.[13]

Carruth praises the blues stanza's potential as a verse form, not a musical structure. To his chagrin, though, American poets favor other verse forms. "Many will remember," Carruth notes, writing in 1985, "when, fifteen or so years back, the classical Persian ghazal seized the imagination of American poets like Adrienne Rich and Jim Harrison and others. Fine work was done, at least in part because some foundation or other offered fellowships for translations from the ghazals of Mirza Ghalib. But how could these poets resort to a kind of poetry so remote and alien, and not give at least equal attention to the only major kind of poetry invented in our own country and our own time? The blues are not only expressive, they are ours" (Carruth, "Blues as Poetry," 298). Carruth employs a rhetoric of possession. American poets own the blues; "they are ours." His comments continue American criticism's long tradition of framing questions of poetic form in nationalistic terms. According to Carruth, a culture's possession of a form entails certain obligations. American poets should concentrate on the forms "invented in our own country and our own time," not a "remote and alien" form such as the ghazal.

Ironically, Carruth's logic suggests why white American poets gravitated to the ghazal, not the blues. The rhetoric of possession also guides the blues' critical reception. Yet the key terms are racial, not, as Carruth wishes, nationalistic. *"The song and the people is the same"* (his italics), Baraka wrote, defining the blues as the "racial memory."[14] By "people," of course he meant Black, not American.

As Baraka's comments suggest, especially in the 1960s the blues signified blackness at its most undiluted and authentic. The period's burgeoning blues scholarship echoes the Black Aesthetic's insistence on "the blues as an expression of 'differentness,'" "an expression of the separateness of the two racial groups."[15] Stephen Henderson fine-tunes this formulation:

> Surely some structures are more distinctly Black, more recognizably Black, than others. Thus the three-line blues form is more distinctly Black than a sonnet by Claude McKay, for example. The ballad, because it is a form (in the Anglo-American tradition) which was early appropriated by Blacks—on both folk and formal levels—is also more definitely "Black" than the sonnet. But the blues, an invention of Black people, is "Blacker" than both.[16]

Fraed by this rhetoric of possession, a white writer's use of "black" forms constitutes larceny, not homage; it invites comparisons to the music industry's many exploitations of black musicians, not mutually beneficial cross-racial commerce. Keenly aware of this history, the Black Aesthetic asserted that Black culture's survival depended on resisting these appropriations. Arguing the opposite point as Carruth, Ron Wellburn employs a similar rhetoric of possession, asking that the Black Aesthetic movement be judged on "the extent to which we are able to control our culture, and specifically our music, from theft and exploitation by aliens" (Gayle, *Black Aesthetic*, 132–33).

Given this context, the blues remained a too "distinctively black" art form for Rich to appropriate without defeating the strategy her ghazals develop. A blues verse would re-invoke the very differences that distinguish her from Baraka. Any mistake would offer an easy occasion for ridicule; a misstep would be read as a sign of cultural ignorance, a confirmation that, as Samuel Charters asserts, "No one could listen to the blues without realizing that there are two Americas."[17]

Almost immediately Rich's example proved influential. Since her sequences' publication, American poets started to write ghazals, with many writers specifically crediting her work as their inspiration. In addition to Harrison's *Outlyer and Ghazals,* Rich's influence can be seen in John Thompson's book-length sequence *Stilt Jack* (1978) and Denise Levertov's "Broken Ghazals."[18] Many of the ghazals that followed Rich's show little knowledge of the form beyond her adaptations. Usually consisting of at least five unrhymed, metrically irregular couplets, they would be impossible to identify as "ghazals" if their titles did not identify them as such.

During the last decade, the ghazal underwent a remarkable transformation that reversed the direction of metrical forms' typical development. During this period, metrical structures tended to allow greater permissiveness and flexibility. As we have seen, poets wrote "free-verse sestinas" or works in this form that used rhyme or anagram substitutions, not the traditional word repetition. In contrast, the ghazal, which started in America as a largely free-verse structure, has recently tended to incorporate more of its traditional rhyme and stanzaic features.

The main figure behind this movement has been Agha Shahid Ali, a poet, translator, anthologist, and essayist, who has mounted a campaign for "the Persian model" as "the real thing."[19] Ali has composed many poems in this form, written several widely noticed essays on "the ghazal in America," and edited an anthology, *Ravishing DisUnities: Real Ghazals in English* (2000).[20] A self-professed "triple exile" from New Delhi, Ali moved to Kashmir as a child then to the United States, where he has lived since 1976. After Ali's death in December 2001, his literary trust oversaw the publication of *Call Me Ishmael Tonight: A Book of Ghazals* (2003), a book that solidified Ali's identification with the form. His gradual attraction to the ghazal form expresses the complicated politics of exile inflected in formal poetic terms.

Ali did not start publishing ghazals until he had lived in America for more than a decade, even though he enjoyed an enviably rich early introduction to this verse tradition. Faiz Ahmed Faiz, an Urdu poet and one of the form's masters, visited Ali's family in Kashmir; his parents and grandmother recited Faiz's verse to him and he heard ghazals sung in performance.[21] Ali's first four volumes of poetry respectfully mention "ghazals weary with ancient images," yet they employ other forms, mainly free verse.[22]

First published in 1997, Ali's "Ghazal I" provides a vivid example of how his prosodic choices dramatize his tangled literary and cultural loyalties. Dedicated "for Edward W. Said," the poem employs a dauntingly elaborate version of the ghazal:

In Jerusalem a dead phone's dialed by exiles.
You learn your strange fate: you were exiled by exiles.

You open the heart to list unborn galaxies.
Don't shut that folder when Earth is filed by exiles.

Before Night passes over the wheat of Egypt,
let stones be leavened, the bread torn wild by exiles.

Crucified Mansoor was alone with the Alone:
God's loneliness—just His—compiled by exiles.

By the Hudson lies Kashmir, brought from Palestine—
It shawls the piano, Bach beguiled by exiles.

Tell me who's tonight the Physician of Sick Pearls?
Only you as you sit, Desert Child, by exiles.

Match Majnoon (he kneels to pray on a wine-stained rug)
or prayer will be nothing, distempered mild by exiles.

"Even things that are true can be proved." Even they?
Swear not by Art but, O Oscar Wilde, by exiles.

Don't weep, we'll drown out the Calls to Prayer, O Saqi—
I'll raise my glass before wine is defiled by exiles.

Was—after the last sky—this the fashion of fire:
Autumn's mist pressed to ashes styled by exiles?

If my enemy's alone and his arms are empty,
give him my heart silk-wrapped like a child by exiles.

Will you, Beloved Stranger, ever witness Shahid—
two destinies at last reconciled by exiles?[23]

Ali's prosody implicitly criticizes Rich's. In his many essays on the subject, Ali describes how American ignorance of the ghazal tradition constitutes "an insult to a very significant element of my culture" (Ali, *Rebel's Silhouette*, xiii) and how "[m]any American poets (the list is surprisingly long) have either misunderstood or ignored the form, and those who have followed them have accepted *their* examples to represent the real thing" (Ali, *Ravishing DisUnities*, 2). Employing the rhetoric of cultural possession, Ali often quotes his own poetry to illustrate "the real thing," the "authentic" ghazal, and its requisite formal features. In "Ghazal I," Ali's prosody accomplishes similar pedagogical functions, strictly defining the form. The first couplet fixes the ghazal's pattern. Ending both lines, "by exiles" establishes itself as the poem's radif, the phrase that ends every subsequent couplet's final line. "[D]ialed" and "exiled" introduce the root-rhyme for the qafia, the rhyme that every word immediately preceding "by exiles" continues. Following the ghazal's traditional pattern, the next three couplets rhyme "dialed" and "exiled" with "filed," "wild," and "compiled."

As if these severe restrictions were inadequate, Ali adds another, one that the ghazal form does not demand. "Ghazal I" rhymes the radif, "by exiles," and the qafia, the root-rhyme of "dialed" and "exiled":

> In Jerusalem a dead phone's dialed by exiles.
> You learn your strange fate: you were exiled by exiles.

"[E]xiled by exiles" forms the poem's key phrase, as all of its rhymes arise from the double rhyme.

This prosodic flourish pays homage to the poem's addressee and dedicatee, Edward Said. "[T]he most poignant of exile's fates," Said observed in a phrase that the poem borrows, "is to be exiled by exiles, and to be condemned, seemingly without respite, to continue to be exiled by exiles. . . . Exile begets exile."[24] The ghazal's prosody embodies this idea. This rhyme of "exiled" and "by exiles" acts as a generative device; with each occurrence "[e]xile begets exile." Organizing the poem, this "strange fate" dominates it, as each couplet reminds the reader of exile's relentless progress, encompassing "wild" and "mild," "beguiled" and "defiled," the English aesthete "Oscar Wilde" and a "Desert child." The farther the monorhyme moves from its original phrase, the more it suggests exile's omnipresence. Just as the poem imagines exiles spreading throughout the "Earth" to "unborn galaxies," the twelve rhymes of "exiled," coupled with the twelve repetitions of "by exiles," radiate this phrase through the poem.

While Ali's handling of the ghazal form marks the wide dispersions that exile performs, it also exerts a counterforce to these same forces. Employing the full length that the canonical form allows, the twelve stanzas gather a community of exiles, based on the values of forgiveness and mutual trust. "Swear not by Art but, O Oscar Wilde, by exiles," the poem counsels:

> If my enemy's alone and his arms are empty,
> give him my heart silk-wrapped like a child by exiles.
>
> Will you, Beloved Stranger, ever witness Shahid—
> two destinies at last reconciled by exiles?

Earlier in his poetic career, Ali satirized the conventional imagery of classical Kashmiri ghazals, "[t]he inevitable moth and *bulbul*."[25] "Ghazal I" instead employs Ali's favorite pun, which another of his conclusions more directly presents. In lines fated to serve as his epitaph, Ali declares:

> They ask me to tell them Shahid means—
> Listen: It means "The Beloved" in Persian, "witness" in Arabic.[26]

This pun complicates the question that the final couplet poses. The final couplet of "Ghazal I" can be read as a cry of anguish, a lamentation over the seemingly endless nature of exile. In this sense, the answer to the rhetorical question it poses is "No." In another sense, the final couplet presents an idealized model for reconciliation. With its knotty grammar and syntax, the final lines suggest that "to witness" is to "reconcile"; exile need not be endless because a possible solution exists. If the different exiles can witness each others' "destinies," the cycle of "[e]xile beget[ting] exile" might stop. Through their mutually sustaining acts of witness, Said, a Palestinian-American, and Ali, an exile from New Delhi and Kashmir, provide an alternative model to the violence that ravages their homelands.

The pun further personalizes this grand hope. As in many canonical ghazals, the nature of the relationship between the speaker and addressee remains ambiguous, leaving unresolved basic questions such as whether the speaker is a disciple addressing God or a poet beseeching his beloved, and, if the latter, whether the beloved is male or female.[27] "Ghazal I" pursues another option: that the poet addresses himself or, to be more precise, the "destinies" that exile imposes on him. As with the poem's rhyme scheme, Ali accepts a basic requirement of the ghazal—the inclusion of a penname in the final stanza—and adds another level of difficulty. The penultimate line of "Ghazal I" mentions three variations of Ali's name: an adjective, "Beloved," a verb, "witness," and a noun, "Shahid." By doing so, Ali uses the ghazal form both to suggest that exile's "destinies" remain irreconcilable and to reconcile them.

"Where rhyme seems to reflect grand harmonies," Debra Fried notes, "pun indicates grand confusions."[28] Though many exceptions challenge this generalization, it neatly describes the final couplet. The puns present language as a Babel of conflicting meanings, where the same sounds signify radically different ideas. Like his name, the poet exists among and between these various meanings and the cultures they represent. At the same time, though, the final couplet harmonizes these meanings to make grammatical, syntactical, and prosodic sense; together, they elegantly solve the problems the verse form presents. The poem's last rhyme completes this process, transforming "exiled" into "reconciled."

In short, "Ghazal I" uses the ghazal form to express exile's contradictions, the particular hopes and despairs that a secular Muslim exile experiences, kneeling on "a wine-stained rug" to pray. Like Rich, Ali writes a transnational poetry of witness, but he reconfigures the triangulation of difference that she employs. As we have seen, Rich invokes Ghalib to shorten the distance between herself and Baraka. Ali's stricter prosody distinguishes his poetry from the "so-called ghazals" that American poets such as Rich and Harrison write (Ali, *Ravishing DisUnities*, 11). Exceeding the form's canonical requirements, "Ghazal I" sharpens the contrast between it and the American versions.

Ali contrasts his efforts with Rich's in order to shorten the distance between himself and fellow exiles, to construct a poetry of exile, a community based in a shared experience. This "strange fate" overrides geopolitical differences, allowing Ali to place "Kashmir" "[b]y the Hudson," "brought from Palestine." While Rich contends with Baraka's violently anti-Semitic and homophobic declarations, Ali uses the ghazal form to smooth over other uncomfortable facts. The form's long, rich history in several languages, including Urdu, Arabic, Turkish, and Persian, elides the significant differences between the forms of exile that he and Said experience. This context also promotes Said as a man of peace, hope, and forgiveness, not a fiery opponent of the Oslo peace agreement once photographed hurling a stone at an Israeli guardhouse.[29]

Like Rich, Ali immediately influenced the ghazal's development. In 2001 several of his friends organized a ghazal chain, "Ghazal for Shahid (Missing You in Palm Springs, 2001)," as a "communal tribute"[30] when he was too ill to attend the Associated Writing Programs' annual conference, held in Palm Springs, where he was scheduled to give a reading. Visitors read two versions of the poem to Ali while he suffered from his illness; the poem continued to expand after his death until its published version contained eighty-three couplets, each composed by a different poet.

Even more than the ghazal chain, the anthology that Ali edited demonstrates his influence on American poets' notion of the form. Like several of the other included poems, John Haag's "Ghazal" directly address Ali, playfully chiding him:

> Oh Shahid, you've treated me cruelly—such mad
> intractable forms, when I write, cause fevers.
>
> (Ali, *Ravishing DisUnities*, 67)

Many of the other poems similarly cast the ghazal as a "mad / intractable form," a relentless producer of language. With "language" as its radif, Daniel Hall's "Souvenir" uses "language" to generate language, forbidding only the unadorned phrase. One couplet offers a group *ars poetica*:

> Plain speech? There's no such thing! I can't tell you
> how much the overwrought can undergird in my language.
>
> (Ibid., 70)

This punningly "overwrought" verse turns the ghazal into a postmodern word game, a means to flaunt and inspect language's mysteries.

The anthology's most suggestive poem departs from this model, offering a silence after long speech. Consisting of just one couplet more than the required five, Carole Stone's "Royal" presents a deceptively quiet drama:

> We are one of those long-married couples who do not speak.
> Especially after our argument on the train to Brighton, we do not speak.
>
> For the life of me, I can't read a timetable, while my husband can.
> Around us, elderly couples lift pasty faces to sun, and do not speak.
>
> I order Earl Grey with milk and sugar, and creme-filled biscuits.
> Reclining on green and white-striped lawn chairs, we still do not speak.
>
> We visit the Royal Palace where King George IV summered.
> I wonder if, like exhausted marrieds, kings and queens do not speak.
>
> Among regal objects d'art, were they ever pierced through the heart?
> Or suffer emotional pains about which the English do not speak?
>
> I, Carole, an American, understand little of royal restraint.
> I am myself a ruined soul, with wild fantasies I do not speak.
>
> (Ibid., 150)

"Too volatile, am I?" Heather McHugh's ghazal demands, "too voluble? Too much a word-person?" (ibid., 113) "Royal" might ask if it remains too restrained, too reticent. It domesticates the ghazal, presenting a unified scene that forgoes the canonical form's fragmentary argumentative structure. The poem seeks stability in a form that often inspires near-frenetic movement. It eliminates the qafia and varies as little as possible the radif, never reversing its meaning or even substantially revising it. Instead of culminating with a wildly punning conclusion, "Royal" builds to an anticonfession, a revelation of what the poem will not reveal, the "wild fantasies I do not speak." Even the penname could not be plainer: "Carole," simply the poet's first name.

"Royal" lacks the large political imperatives that drive Rich's and Ali's ghazals. It slyly uses this form to evoke the strangeness an outsider feels: an American traveling in England, a wife suffering an uncommunicative marriage. Unlike Rich, Stone does not seek to translate her age's historical fissures into prosodic terms. Her wry, quietly elegant ghazal instead confirms that the form has entered a new stage of its development in America. It need not address subjects too explosive to approach directly, but quotidian moments barely worth mentioning. Hinting at more than it names, "Royal" marks both a trivialization and an opening of the field.

THREE

WHEN A FORM COMES OUT
OF THE CLOSET

IS GREAT LOVE LITERATURE STILL POSSIBLE? EVERY DAY PEOPLE FALL IN love, but shrewd readers report they no longer take seriously Western literature's major theme. Why?

The experience of romantic love involves the intense feeling of extraordinariness, a sense that the two who share it are uniquely suited for each other, "soul mates," as the cliché goes. For this reason, one cannot love just anyone. Classic love literature places this desire as the key to self-understanding, to a life passionately lived. Many contemporary readers are far too suspicious to accept such a claim, except ironically. The experience of love, they know, is hardly unprecedented; even when a novel or a poem asserts that the depicted love affair makes the characters extraordinary, the artistic form confirms that the declaration follows a well-established literary convention. The lovers are as ordinary as the emotion they experience. This situation's awkwardness defines "the postmodern temper," as Umberto Eco argues: "I think of the postmodern attitude as that of a man who loves a very cultivated woman and knows he cannot say to her, 'I love you madly,' because he knows that she knows (and that she knows that he knows) that these words have already been written by Barbara Cartland."[1] "These words have already been written by Barbara Cartland," the "Queen of Romance," not a poet or novelist: after all, love remains an important subject for romance novels and Hollywood comedies. The present age demands the strategies of "irony, metalinguistic play, enunciation squared" to accept love as a linguistic and philosophical game (ibid., 68). But classic love literature requires the innocence that Eco believes to be lost: a moment when cynicism breaks into a kind of transcendent belief, where others' words are no longer quoted but sensation is experienced as an overpowering, transforming truth.

Given these difficulties, it is tempting to follow Vivian Gornick's bold declaration that we have reached "the end of the novel of love." In a provocative and subtle argument, she calls "love as a metaphor" "an act of nostalgia, not of discovery."[2] Over the last forty years, the breakdown of sexual and marital taboos has led to a different understanding of what constitutes self-knowledge:

> Certainly, it [love] can no longer act as an organizing principle. Romantic love now seems a yearning to dive down into feeling and come up magically changed; when what is required for the making of a self is the deliberate pursuit of consciousness. Knowing *this* to be the larger truth, as many of us do, the idea of love as a means of illumination—in literature as in life—now comes as something of an anticlimax. (Ibid., 162)

"We all know too much" to take these worn-out myths seriously and the novels that repeat them as if they were still operative. Thus, the novel of love has declined into a convention without vitality, unrooted in the way its readers live, "the equivalent of living in bad faith" (ibid., 163).

If the novel of love is "dead," the love sonnet should also be mourned, buried with the Petrarchan conventions that generations of readers have ridiculed: "the place" (in Robert Bly's quip) where "old professors go when they die."[3] Indeed, for decades the love sonnet has seemed artistically exhausted. Although poets have continued to write love sonnets, the weight of the form's Petrarchan past largely outstrips its benefits. Writing in an age skeptical of Petrarchan traditions, too often contemporary sonneteers settle for either an untenable optimism or a tentative defensiveness.

Faced with these conceptual and formal difficulties, a group of writers has found exceptional solutions. During the last two decades, gay and lesbian poets have dominated the art of the love sonnet. In addition to a host of less notable works, they have written some of the most distinguished and widely admired poems in this form, among them, Marilyn Hacker's book-length sequence *Love, Death, and the Changing of the Seasons* (1986), the sonnets in Rafael Campo's *The Other Man Was Me* (1993) and *What the Body Told* (1996), Henri Cole's *The Look of Things* (1995) and *The Visible Man* (1998), and examples throughout James Merrill's many volumes. As one of Campo's sonnets on the sonnet announces, the form has been rewritten as "queer."[4]

The reasons for this development are numerous—some genre specific, some not. Gays and lesbians have contributed to American culture new definitions of love, challenging common notions of family, marriage, sexual desire, and intimacy. Longer and more intensely than any others, they have faced the challenge of AIDS. Despite Gornick's sense that bourgeois taboos have passed, gays and lesbians still endure the threat of violence and other, less aggressive forms of discrimination. Drawing upon these experiences, gay and lesbian authors continue to revitalize the love novel. Most famously Michael Cunningham's *The Hours* movingly explores what it means "to love singularly, over the decades, against all reason."[5] Gay and lesbian writers of love sonnets also draw from the form's particular literary-historical resources. They discover how the form's Petrarchan conventions uncannily echo the complex cultural, psychic, and material conditions of contemporary gay and lesbian life.

This striking alliance of "traditional" prosody and "radical" scholarship has yet to receive the attention it deserves. Too often assumed to be the sign of aesthetic and political conservatism, metrical verse garners little consideration in critical discussions of "queer poetics" as the project to "imagine" "new forms." Contradicting such positions, an individual work such as Hacker's *Love, Death, and the Changing of the Seasons* is typically referred to as a "notable exception" to larger formal trends.[6] When read as a group, not exceptions, these love sonnets allow a more accurate account of not only contemporary gay and lesbian poetry but the nature of metrical composition.

Loudly calling for a return to metrical verse, many poets and scholars associated with new formalism assert that contemporary scholarship's interest in identity studies contributes to a widespread ignorance of poetic technique. In a complaint that echoes others by scholars outside the movement as different as Denis Donoghue, Marjorie Perloff, and John Hollander, Timothy Steele insists that "[c]lassifying poetry by the causes it addresses," such as "'gay activists,' 'native Americans,' 'black poets,' and so forth," "trivializes meter: the practice confuses what is extrinsic to poetic structure with what is intrinsic to it."[7] Yet, as the love sonnets that I will discuss show, a poet's formal handling of poetic structure involves a host of aesthetic, cultural, political, and technical considerations; in Steele's terms, it already "confuses" the "extrinsic" with the "intrinsic." To overlook this fact is to trivialize the complex functions poetic form accomplishes.

On Not Living in a Sonnet World

> For past objects have about them past necessities—like the sonnet—which have conditioned them and from which, as a form itself, they cannot be freed.
>
> The poem being an object (like a symphony or cubist painting) it must be the purpose of the poet to make of his words a new form: to invent, that is, an object consonant with his day.
>
> We do not live in a sonnet world.
>   —William Carlos Williams,
>   *The Autobiography of William Carlos Williams*

> [W]e have stopped making formal declarations of love.
>   —Denis de Rougemont, *Love in the Western World*

Over the course of Western literary history, no other verse form can claim the sonnet's popularity, its influence, or its fame. In *The Birth of the Modern Mind: Self, Consciousness, and the Invention of the Sonnet* (1989), Paul Oppenheimer goes so far as to argue that "[m]odern thought and literature begin with the invention of the sonnet," an event which he dates in the early thirteenth century. According to Oppenheimer, the sonnet signaled a new inwardness, a heightened sense of self-consciousness and internal division. Thus, "the first lyric of self-consciousness, or of the self in conflict" helped achieve "the birth of the modern mind."[8]

While the sonnet is the most famous poetic form, love is its most well-known subject. Because love sonnets generally adhere to a predetermined metrical form and subject matter, both of these elements belong to a recognizable tradition. With these requirements added to the form's distinguished history, a contemporary sonneteer's need to balance literary originality and precedent grows particularly acute.

Indeed, love sonnets revise a very particular kind of love: the codified and ritualized processes of Petrarchan courtship. Such verse conventions, established by Dante and Petrarch and translated into English by Wyatt and Surrey, mark the origin of the form in English and its evolution. Among these traditions are specific themes and tropes, or what Leonard Forster calls "the petrarchistic idiom [that] became the obligatory language of love."[9] As Forster notes, the most prominent themes are "praise of the lady," "the effect the beloved produces on the lover," the relationship's "constant state of delicious fluidity," and the uniqueness of the depicted love (ibid., 9, 13, 15). The tropes that traditionally help express these themes are the "blason" (the ritualistic, highly metaphoric praising of the beloved's body), wit, hyperbole, and antithesis, all of which reflect the extremity of the depicted emotional states. Although these themes and tropes commonly work in concert, they need not do so and can be used in opposition. To cite the most famous example of anti-Petrarchan Petrarchanism, Shakespeare's Sonnet 130 employs anti-Petrarchan tropes to express a stock Petrarchan theme: the singularity of his love.[10]

Sonnet 130 also highlights the ambivalence many Renaissance love sonneteers felt toward the courtly traditions they inherited. Since the Renaissance, changing attitudes toward love and literary tradition intensified this ambivalence about Petrarchan conventions into a more pervasive and severe skepticism. The period between 1500 and 1800 witnessed great changes in the public's attitudes toward love, marriage, and literature. In the late 1800s the rise of "companionate marriages"—that is, marriages based on principles of shared love and friendship—superseded the previous standard of matrimony motivated largely by economic factors. Although the historian Lawrence Stone concedes that "cause and effect is . . . impossible to resolve," he also notes that "romantic love and the romantic novel grew together after 1780 . . . romantic love became a respectable motive for marriage among the propertied classes, and that at the same time there was a rising flood of novels filling the shelves of the circulating libraries, devoted to the same theme."[11] In contrast to the aristocratic, often adulterous romances depicted in many sonnet sequences, early novels tended to celebrate love within marriages, not outside them. While Renaissance sonneteers circulated their work primarily through courtly circles, a growing bourgeois readership, supported by lending libraries, formed the novel's main audience. The novel offered this emerging audience new images and definitions of love in return for a popularity and an influence that other genres could only envy. If, as Peter Gay observes, "Committed to contemporary realities, the modern novel could scarcely overlook the bourgeois and his loves," the opposite also is true: the bourgeois and his loves could scarcely overlook the novel.[12]

Modernism added another assault on the love sonnet's status. Positing a distinction between poetry and rhetoric that would have puzzled Renaissance writers, Modernist poets eschewed conspicuously employed classical tropes and schemes. The poet should "[t]ake rhetoric and wring its neck," not labor to master it as the demonstration of cultivated intelligence and learning.[13] An exercise Pound set at his "Ezuversity" in Rapallo neatly illustrates this attitude. Pound assigned Basil Bunting the task of editing Shakespeare's sonnets, cutting out the "superfluous words." Bunting pared Sonnet 87 to two lines.[14]

It is telling that Pound chose a sonnet for Bunting to rewrite. There is nothing intrinsically "rhetorical" about a sonnet; a free-verse poem might contain as many classical figures and tropes as a sonnet, if not more. However, inspired by their distaste for Victorian verse's excesses, many leading Modernists conflated poetic styles with specific metrical forms.[15] Hulme, for instance, insisted that "[r]egular metre" "introduces the heavy, crude pattern of rhetorical verse."[16] Eliot, who similarly declared that "revolution[s] in idiom . . . bring with them an alteration of metric," voiced doubts that even a "man of genius" could rehabilitate the sonnet.[17] However, it was Williams, the Modernist most committed to the contemporary idiom, who offered the most categorical dismissals. In Williams's essays and letters, the sonnet regularly symbolizes all he finds objectionable in metrical verse. Thus, Williams believed that the "thoroughly banal" sonnet form "cannot be freed" from its past and should be shunned in favor of "new forms."[18]

More recent changes in gender relations intensified the love sonnet's trivialization. Feminist social and literary criticism has called much attention to the power disparities at work in Renaissance courtship rituals; read in this light, the romances depicted in many love sonnets embody some of the culture's worst attitudes. Some readers' "skepticism" grows so profound as to question whether the love sonnet may be unredeemable, as the form's past threatens to overpower even revisionist attempts to rewrite it. Margaret Homans's "'Syllables of Velvet': Dickinson, Rossetti, and the Rhetorics of Sexuality" (1985) argues that Petrarchan love sonnets act out "the plot of masculine, heterosexual desire" that dominates "the romantic lyric."[19] According to Homans, the legacy of Petrarchan conventions puts female poets in a particularly dangerous position:

> The romantic lyric, then, with its concentrated plot of heterosexual desire and its heavy reliance on specular metaphor, simply intensified for women writers and readers a difficulty that could perhaps be evaded in other literary forms, such as the novel. Given a literary form constructed so clearly to the specifications of male desire, women writers did not often choose to write romantic lyrics, for to do so was either to repeat the traditional quest plot, in linguistic drag, or to take up the position of the silent object and its attempt to speak from there. (Ibid., 573–74)

For Homans, a female poet such as Christina Rossetti who writes a strategically anti-Petrarchan sonnet sequence dooms herself to failure because "in the end tradition writes her perhaps as much as she rewrites tradition" (ibid., 574). Indeed, although Homans cites Dickinson as a notable exception, her general rule is that female poets who express "heterosexual desire" with "specular metaphors" celebrate the very traditions that oppress them.

Homans's argument exemplifies a certain critical tendency to consider the sonnet as a largely static form. Although critiquing what she calls "the lyric's" claim to "ahistoricity," she posits that "the Petrarchan love lyric," "the lyric," "the romantic lyric," and pretty much all of Western culture smoothly progress from the early Italian Renaissance to the contemporary age. All express "conventions of male sexuality that *operate continuously* in our culture, from Petrarch's day to our own" (ibid., 572; my italics). Arguments more specific to the sonnet repeat this assumption of basic continuity. "Because the sonnet has changed very little over the seven centuries of its life," a recent study of the form begins.[20]

The sonnet, on the contrary, has changed greatly. Historical periods substantially disagree over its formal properties, themes, central writers, cultural functions, and artistic challenges. In the Augustan age, the sonnet barely existed; between 1700 and 1755 fewer than one hundred sonnets were printed in England.[21] By Doctor Johnson's definition, the form was "not very suitable to the English language, and has not been used by any man of eminence since Milton."[22] Even though the contemporary age sees Shakespeare's sequence as almost self-evidently central to the form's history, eighteenth-century editors thought so little of these sonnets that they proudly excluded them from their editions of Shakespeare's works. "We have not reprinted the Sonnets," George Steevens explained, "because the strongest act of Parliament that could be framed, could not compel readers into their service."[23] Indeed, both eighteenth- and nineteenth-century readers preferred Milton's sonnets as a triumphant alternative to Petrarchan love.

The eighteenth century, though an extreme example, underscores the sonnet's instability. Although contemporary standards consider the love sonnet to be the most traditional form's most traditional expression, Augustan neoclassicism regarded it as foreign and tasteless. Indeed, the trivialization I have referred to is best understand as a series of radically different definitions of "the sonnet." Without such historical grounding, it is too easy to dismiss the form or to praise it for equally untenable reasons.

The contemporary age's particular skepticism about love sonnets can be seen in the work of certain poets who continue to write them. For example, Kate Light's "About Sonnets of Love; Some" grapples with feminist challenges to the love sonnet tradition. Consistent with the poem's comic tone, the sonnet's first line continues the sentence that the title starts:

> complain of us frozen there, a pile
> of praised body parts, objectified;
> bundle of hair and heart and breast and smile;
> killed off line by line, petrified.
> I think it's true the dying of the moments
> begins in their capture—and maybe a man who's
> unable to face his own aging laments
> the woman's, saying *so fades the rose*,
> and like that. Still I sympathize;
> I struggle too with how to praise—
> and yet do not want to advertise—

> or exploit—my lover's secret lovely gaze.
> *Oh elegant beautiful spilling from the cup*
> *of love my love how I could drink you up.*[24]

By referring to "us" who complain about the sonnet's sexist traditions, Light underscores her sympathy for arguments such as Homans's. Her tone when discussing these claims is respectful: "I think it's true," she writes. Indeed, Light voices some of Homans's particular concerns. Just as Homans cites passages from Petrarch's two sonnets, noting "the grim joke that from these two passages one could not tell which sonnet was about a dead woman and which about a living one" (Homans, "Syllables," 571), Light acknowledges how the female characters in sonnets are "killed off line by line, petrified."

At the same time, however, Light clearly cherishes the sonnet tradition's particular tropes: her poem is a blason waiting to happen. In the concluding couplet, "praise" bursts forth:

> *Oh elegant beautiful spilling from the cup*
> *of love my love how I could drink you up.*

In these lines, Light celebrates not only her lover but the idea of sonneteering praise, the *"elegant beautiful spilling from the cup / of love."* The poem works hard to get to this moment of celebration. Italicized for emphasis and set off from the rest of the poem, the couplet needs a two-adjectival phrase to add a kind of grammatical italicization. Even amid this exuberant joy, the sonnet calls attention to its own defensiveness, with twelve conciliatory lines justifying a single couplet of praise. The poem's strength is the shrewdness and humor with which it considers its readers' and its own reservations about Petrarchan traditions. The result, though, only emphasizes the contemporary love sonnet's precarious position, attacked for decades and struggling not to give further offense.

The attention Light's poem devotes to the feminist critique of the Petrarchan love sonnet tradition testifies to this view's currency. As the poem implicitly acknowledges, a love sonneteer cannot afford to ignore such skepticism. This point is even better illustrated by a much-celebrated love sonnet which does exactly that, Section X of Seamus Heaney's "Glanmore Sonnets":

> I dreamt we slept in a moss in Donegal
> On turf banks under blankets, with our faces
> Exposed all night in a wetting drizzle,
> Pallid as the dripping sapling birches.
> Lorenzo and Jessica in a cold climate.
> Diarmuid and Grainne waiting to be found.
> Darkly asperged and censed, we were laid out
> Like breathing effigies on a raised ground.
> And in that dream I dreamt—how like you this?—
> Our first night years ago in that hotel
> When you came with your deliberate kiss
> To raise us towards the lovely and painful
> Covenants of flesh; our separateness;
> The respite in our dewy dreaming faces.[25]

Heaney's sonnet breaks with Petrarch's own practices but does so within the larger Petrarchan tradition. Unlike Petrarch and Laura, the poet and his lover consummate their relationship. According to Petrarchan convention, though, the lovers' physical union takes place within a dream.

This example of contemporary Petrarchism calls attention to the impasse the love sonnet faces. Section X culminates in the epiphany of the two young lovers' "separateness." This insight is a plausible and even poignant revelation for lovers to experience on their "first night"; that is, they are startled to find that their sexual union reveals an intensity beyond ordinary experience. The poet and his beloved experience a vision of what the philosopher Irving Singer calls "the idealist tradition of love." "[R]aise[d] . . . towards the lovely and painful / Covenants of flesh," the two lovers enter a mythologized, metaphysical landscape that remakes them into "a single oneness that is their merged condition."[26] However, the poem offers this revelation as an epiphany not only to the lovers but also to the reader. For this insight to work as an epiphany, a sudden, unexpected moment of truth, the reader must accept it as a new discovery, not a cliché.

As suggested by the sardonic self-portrait of "Lorenzo and Jessica in a cold climate," the perceptions of the mature speaker and his younger self work in dramatic tension. The poem, though, ultimately fails because the self-knowledge it possesses and the naïveté it claims stand in radical opposition. The sonnet's many literary references to Shakespeare, Wyatt, and Irish legend acknowledge that the views it presents firmly belong to idealistic love's long poetic and cultural tradition. Yet, after quoting learned precedents out of beautiful old books, the sonnet cannot bring itself to admit the obvious: that, as even Yeats, one of "the last romantics," ruefully acknowledged, this "old high way of love" is no longer culturally or artistically viable.[27] In short, the "Glanmore Sonnet" pursues a self-defeating strategy, pretending to know less than its readers.

Queering the Sonnet

> Seriously and solemnly Richard Dalloway got on his hind legs and said that no decent man ought to read Shakespeare's sonnets because it was like listening at keyholes (besides the relationship was not one that he approved).
>
> Virginia Woolf, *Mrs. Dalloway*

"It won't do just yet," W. H. Auden campily warned in 1964, "to admit that the top Bard belonged to the homintern."[28] Two decades later, after Stonewall and amid the AIDS epidemic, it was time. Along with Joseph Pequigney's *Such Is My Love: A Study of Shakespeare's Sonnets*" (1985), Eve Kosofsky Sedgwick's often-cited "Swan in Love: The Example of Shakespeare's Sonnets" in *Between Men: English Literature and Male Homosocial Desire* (also published in 1985) changed the terms of Shakespeare scholarship from what Pequigney calls "the problem of protecting the work and its author from the embarrassment and scandal of homosexuality" to a more frank assessment of the erotic entanglements that the sonnets depict.[29] Even though Sedgwick and Pequigney categorize this dynamic differently, their work established what now seems a blandly obvious point: that "Shakespeare [in the Sonnets] produced not only extraordinary amatory verse but the grand masterpiece of homoerotic poetry."

Inspired by this "queering of the Renaissance," teaching practices changed.[30] Even a reader as sophisticated as David H. Richter confessed that, when previously teaching the Sonnets, he had employed "ethically questionable" and "intellectually dishonest" techniques such as directing the "students to imagine the sonnet [under discussion] is addressed to a woman if they can't cope." Shamed by Sedgwick's work, Richter renounced these methods.

In addition to this local effect, queer studies broadcast the question of Shakespeare's sexuality beyond a specialist audience. Soon the question of Shakespeare's sexuality turned into a controversy familiar to many students before they entered college. As John Crowe Ransom recounts, some of his students were "frightened" and others disgusted when they "suddenly discovered that the face which Shakespeare adored was that of a man."[31] Only two decades later, professors who teach the Sonnets must be prepared for their already-informed students to ask, "Was Shakespeare gay?"[32]

One of queer studies' less predictable influences has been on the writing of metrical verse. While previous generations of gay and lesbian poets decried the sonnet as "too untrue" and "patriarchal" to express their experiences, gay and lesbian poets writing in the eighties and nineties recognized the form as crucial to gay and lesbian literary history.[33] Queer studies' reinterpretation of Shakespeare's Sonnets played an important role in this process. Calling attention to how desperately many influential readers tried to explain away what Coleridge called Shakespeare's "very worst of all possible Vices," it recast the sonnet as an obvious vehicle for gay and lesbian desire.[34] For some younger poets in the 1980s, this scholarship formed an important part of their intellectual training; others experienced the work only as a cultural controversy. For a poet such as Marilyn Hacker, a dedicated reader of queer theory already expressing lesbian sexuality in metrical forms, queer theory placed her work within a longer tradition of gay and lesbian literature, confirming her belief that "traditional" forms need not advance reactionary politics.[35]

In some cases, queer studies directly influenced poets' formal choices. In "The Fairiest College" in The Poetry of Healing: A Doctor's Education in Empathy, Identity, and Desire (1997), Rafael Campo describes how the class he took with Sedgwick changed his life. For Campo, who, like the other gay and lesbian students at Amherst, felt "invisible except at those painful moments when we were made the objects of bigotry," Sedgwick's class was like "putting on a slinky strapless cocktail dress—I was preparing to feel desirable again." "[U]nder the influence of Eve Sedgwick, whose instruction, as any of her students will report, is the most potent of all aphrodisiacs[,] I wrote poetry feverishly. . . . By the time Valentine's Day was nearly arrived, my plan had come to me in the form of a sonnet."[36] In the sonnet that Campo wrote, he came out to his best friend and future partner, announcing his love: "All that I had learned was contained neatly on a small square card, in fourteen lines that sang with my heart and rhymed with my sobs. I had made my honest declaration of love" (ibid., 99). According to Campo's account, the sonnet provided him with the formal means to offer an "honest declaration of love" not only to his future lover but to himself. The class with Sedgwick and the sonnet form worked together to help the previously closeted poet express his love amid Amherst's repressive climate.

Given the role that the sonnet played in one of the central moments in Campo's life, it is unsurprising that he returns to this form almost obsessively. In *What the Body Told,* Campo constructs a lineage of gay sonneteers, referring to Shakespeare's and Michelangelo's sequences, and converting Elizabeth Barrett Browning's "Sonnets from the Portuguese" into "Sonnet for the Portuguese," a celebration of his male partner. In "Safe Sex," Campo writes:

> Protected in your arms, I dreamed while death
> Passed overhead. I guessed I was alive,
> Because I heard how faintly in your breath
> My name kept being said. We fell in love
> When love was not protection in itself;
> Misled by poetry, I'd always felt
> The pleasures of the tongue were very safe.
> Before your urgent pleading face, I knelt
> To say your love had come to represent
> In me a willingness to die. You came
> Inside my mouth, and eagerly death bent
> Its ear to listen to my heart. The same
> Astonishment without restraint sang out—
> Protected in your arms, I died of doubt.
>   (Campo, *What the Body Told,* 58)

The most common way to reinvigorate an old form is to replace outworn conventions with more contemporary language. A poet might write a Miltonic sonnet in the idiom of a working-class Yorkshireman, as Tony Harrison does in "The School of Eloquence."[37] Campo's Shakespearean sonnet takes the opposite approach. Instead of trying to rid the sonnet of Elizabethan rhetoric, "Safe Sex" employs stock Petrarchisms to startling effect.

In particular, the poem demonstrates how the AIDS crisis adds a new literalness to the most seemingly worn-out Petrarchan trope, the pun of "death," meaning both sexual climax and the absence of life. "Protected in your arms, I died of doubt," the poem ends. This punning line asks to be read in directly contradictory ways. In the line's most optimistic sense, the sexual encounter purges the speaker's doubts. Calmed by his lover's embrace, the speaker enjoys a moment of metaphysical tranquility. In another sense, the sexual climax expresses the speaker's gravest fears, among them, his suspicion that his lover offers him at best the appearance of protection and at worst a deadly disease. Finally and most bleakly, the line also can be read as expressing the speaker's desire for annihilation, not protection. Lying in his lover's arms, he embraces the possibility of infection.

Throughout the form's long history, many love sonnets consider this notion that the sexual instinct simultaneously draws upon a life wish and a death wish. "Safe Sex" expresses this familiar idea in subtle ways, as in its first quatrain's rhyme of "death" with the lover's "breath." The sonnet, though, offers more than an old truth artfully rendered. Set in a contemporary context, this near truism of love sonnets raises a vitally new insight. In his essay "Nor Are We Immune," Campo, an assistant professor of medicine at Harvard Medical School and a physician who regularly treats AIDS patients, considers how he slowly came to accept the disheartening fact that some of his patients actively sought infection. The vast majority of these patients were gay men approximately Campo's age:

> I had yet to understand why anyone might decline to be immune, or how poetry might embody the *refusal* to be saved.
>   I continue to hear from my colleagues, and oftentimes from my own mouth, the automatic refrain that has been our primary response to the epidemic thus far: safe sex, safe sex, safe sex, two seductively alliterative words that would drown out all true poetry. . . . Almost as nullifying as silence itself, the sanitary images and nice bland words we can say in public that seem to be the engines of the public health establishment's representations of AIDS seem to have backfired on all of us. In their place, I have found myself wishing that more poems would be written, in red graffiti spray-painted across billboards—that more rules be broken, that the truth be told. (Campo, *Poetry of Healing*, 188–89)

But how can "the truth be told"? The sonnet form allows Campo two main strategies. First, the "automatic refrain" of "safe sex, safe sex, safe sex" falsifies because it offers the same platitude for nearly all situations. It assumes that people act rationally, even when facing a terrifying epidemic, and that they want sex to be "safe." In contrast, the sonnet form dramatizes the passions of contrary impulses. This point is best illustrated by the following passage:

> Before your urgent pleading face, I knelt
> To say your love had come to represent
> In me a willingness to die. You came
> Inside my mouth, and eagerly death bent
> Its ear to listen to my heart. The same . . .

Especially when compared with other contemporary verse, Campo's meter remains very regular. This passage, for example, includes only one substitution (the fourth line's ionic foot). While this Shakespearean sonnet adheres to the form's rhyme scheme and meter, it diverges from its usual argumentative structure. Instead of ending each quatrain with a complete sentence and thought, the poem almost defiantly concludes every one with the heavily enjambed start of a new sentence. For example, the second quatrain ends and the third begins, "Before your urgent pleading face, I knelt / To say . . ." The effect is that the poem's argument spills from one quatrain to the next; seemingly hurrying to the ensuing thought, the new sentence undercuts the rhyme's sense of formal closure. The passage quoted above mimics this effect by ending each line with an enjambed verb. This technique gives a sense of propulsion, of the speaker's thoughts racing forward almost beyond his control. Just as the speaker longs for both protection and danger, the poem's formal elements tug against each other. A mimesis of the conflicted self, the poem presents rhythms as "urgent" as the lover's "pleading face."

While the sonnet's formal contradictions allow "Safe Sex" to "embody the refusal to be saved," the form as a whole affirms an idealized model of health and sexuality. In "AIDS and the Poetry of Healing," Campo explains his attraction to metrical forms:

> So-called formal poetry holds the most appeal for me because in it are present the fundamental beating contents of the body at peace: the

regularity of resting brain wave activity in contrast to the disorganized
spiking of a seizure, the gentle ebb and flow of breathing, or sobbing,
in contrast to the harsh spasmodic cough, the single-voiced, ringing
chant of a slogan at an ACT UP rally in contrast to the indecipherable
rumblings of AIDS-funding debate on the Senate floor. . . . The poem
perhaps is an idealization, or a dream of the physical—the imagined
healthy form. Yet it does not renounce illness; rather, it reinterprets
it as the beginning point for healing. (Campo, *Poetry of Healing,*
166–67)

In another essay, Campo expands upon this point: "Even if it is not the
miracle cure, the brave, heartfelt poem just might be the safest and most
pleasurable sex of all, providing the kind of empowerment that comes
from fully occupying one's body. . . . It is felt in the heart, in the genitals,
in the mouth and tongue."[38] If Campo's handling of the sonnet form
represents a self wracked by contrary impulses, it also evokes "the body
at peace." As befitting a poet trained in medicine, Campo values poetic
form's biological functions. Thus, the predictability of metrical forms
does not call to his mind "jails" or a metronome's unvarying repetitions
but the workings of a healthy body and body politic.[39]

In "Safe Sex," then, poetic form stages a ritual of healing. Like the
speaker's thoughts, the poem's formal elements skillfully contest each
other; the sonnet form in its entirety, however, represents a sense of
wholeness, of physical and mental well-being. The poem ends:

> The same
> Astonishment without restraint sang out—
> Protected in your arms, I died of doubt.

As in the previous three quatrains, this last quatrain ends with the
enjambed start of a sentence ("The same / Astonishment"). However,
unlike other contemporary poems that use similar devices, "Safe Sex"
does not finish in a moment of disruption, with a sentence fragment
trailing off into a broken thought. Instead, the concluding couplet
resolves the sonnet's grammatical and prosodic complications, as the
final rhyme finishes the poem's last sentence. In the end, each prosodic
element performs its function. The poem's enjambments across
the sonnet's organizational structure evoke a self struggling with its
contentious desires. In contrast, the sonnet form as a whole instills a

comforting sense of well-proportioned order, "a dream of the physical—the imagined healthy form." Thus, poetic form resolves the contrary impulses that in life might be irreconcilable.

Campo is hardly alone in arguing for a biological grounding of metrical verse. However, in contrast to recent polemicists, he makes a point larger than championing metrical verse over free.[40] A major challenge AIDS poses is how sexuality can be expressed joyfully and healthily. In "Safe Sex," Campo submits a radical suggestion. "[F]elt in the heart, in the genitals, in the mouth and tongue," the poem offers an amalgam of the emotional, the erotic, and the sensual. One can easily over-schematize how prosodic elements might correlate to these properties. At the same time, however, it is important to note that, for Campo, poetic form acts as a means for "providing the kind of empowerment that comes from fully occupying one's body." With its arrangement of rhymes, accented and unaccented syllables, the sonnet form engages the body's various senses and faculties. While the poem mocks the simplicities of "safe sex" as an "automatic refrain," it also celebrates verse form as the idealized body where poetry, "the safest and most pleasurable sex of all," can take place.

While Campo's "Safe Sex" praises the love sonnet as a bearer of truth and healing, Henri Cole's "Mesmerism" strategically renounces the comforts that this form offers. Mesmerism consists of two sonnets, the first of which is spoken by the victim and the second by his attacker:

I
Long afterward, people would say blandly,
"Those boys might have done something with their lives."
My suffering didn't frighten them.
I was only a stereotype, waiting
in the snow like a rabbit, asking for life.
It wasn't who but what I was their sons
did not understand as one tethered
my hands behind my head with a necktie.
Weirdly, the pain was comforting—"Take it!"
I thought, "I wish I could give you more"—letting
me know I was alive before I would die.
This was not nobility. I pissed on myself,
groaning aloud, wanting the face
of the sweaty boy who strangled me.

II
Everyone wants to die without pain.
Kneeling before us, with his pretty mouth,
he was a prototype of innocence.
Sweet Jesus, I wanted to hit him. So we did.
Each blow taking us farther than we'd been.
With his neck pulled back, showing the soft front,
and half-naked slender legs, he made me sick.
"I want! I want!" I kept hearing in my head,
without understanding how I was governed
by the thing I'd hated. "I'm just like you,"
he moaned, "I have a mother," which made us laugh.
After the punishment, he lay supine,
as on a china platter. My teeth were foaming.
All that I am was membrane and nails.[41]

"Mesmerism" appears in *The Visible Man*, Cole's most recent collection, whose opening poem, "Arte Povera," another blank-verse sonnet, declares

the end of description & rhyme,
which had nursed and embalmed me at once.
Language was more than a baroque wall-fountain.

(Ibid., 3)

"[D]escription and rhyme" reach their "end" because the poet no longer desires the effects they achieve. He does not want his poetry to be "nursed and embalmed," nurtured at the cost of further experience. Instead, as this sonnet's last line startlingly admits, "My soul-animal prefers the choke-chain." If all forms of writing merely impose different kinds of captivity, the poet's "soul-animal" favors an openly brutal, unadorned "choke-chain," one with little claims to beneficence.

Of course this complaint against "baroque" versification espouses a rather familiar position, echoing an earlier generation's similar pronouncements made during the fifties and sixties. (Even Cole's swipe at Richard Wilbur's "A Baroque Wall-Fountain in Villa Sciarra" sounds a little dated.) Given Cole's views, why, then, write "Mesmerism" as a sonnet? True to Cole's new aesthetic, "Mesmerism" employs a form and a style more austere than his earlier work. The loose blank verse eschews the rhyming skills that his previous volumes parade, and its language grows noticeably coarser. So why not make its lines wholly irregular, expand one section, and condense the other? If the poet seeks freedom from "description & rhyme," why not write free verse, as so many contemporary poets who share these assumptions have done?

Displaying great shrewdness, "Mesmerism" realizes the power of both exploiting and renouncing the sonnet form. Absent the sonnet's traditional rhyme schemes, argumentative organizations, and other recognizable formal properties, the fourteen-line structure marks "Mesmerism" as a sonnet. Mindful of this fact, "Mesmerism" draws an implicit connection between the violence it explores and one of the love sonnet's traditional subjects. As Forster notes, the "classic petrarchistic situation" involves the poet's masochism and the beloved's sadism: "The classic petrarchistic situation is that the lady is hard-hearted; love has struck the poet alone but spared the lady, and he begs that love should strike her too. . . . If there is something of the masochist about the petrarchistic lover, there is something of the sadist in his picture of his beloved" (Forster, *Icy Fire*, 15). The metaphors Forster employs bear an appropriately violent edge; love "has *struck* the poet alone but *spared* the lady and he *begs* that love should *strike her too*" (my italics). While certain sonnets such as Donne's "Batter my heart, three-personed God" dramatize this sado-masochism, the violence they depict remains metaphoric, as the speaker of Donne's poem wants God to rape him figuratively, not literally. "Mesmerism," though, is a Petrarchan love sonnet literalized into actual violence between murderer and victim, not "lady" and "poet." The victim finds himself "wanting the face / of the sweaty boy who strangled me" while the murderer admires the boy's "pretty mouth," "soft front, / and half-naked slender legs." Filled with such images, the poem evokes the dynamic of consensual sado-masochistic sex, as the boy, his hands bound with a necktie, silently urges his attackers to "Take it!" while they inflict the "punishment."

Cole's handling of the sonnet form echoes this sado-masochism. The sonnet form acts as a "choke-chain," guiding the poem by restricting its freedom to go wherever it wants. At the same time, the poem conspicuously denies itself many of the pleasures the sonnet form offers. If any of a large number of other contemporary poets had written "Mesmerism," this loose blank-verse sonnet would seem remarkably "formal." Read in the context of Cole's career, though, "Mesmerism" marks a departure from "description & rhyme," a refusal to be "nursed and embalmed": a drama of deprivation and restraint.

By literalizing the love sonnet's traditional sado-masochistic tropes, "Mesmerism" shows violence and desire to be inextricably intertwined. In the process, the poem captures how homophobic violence often acts out repressed homoerotic desire. For a man to beat to death another man because he is gay is to be "governed / by the thing I'd hated," as the second speaker of "Mesmerism" realizes. Indeed, recent events bear grim evidence of this insight's relevance. According to news reports, Matthew Sheppard's murderers feigned sexual interest in him; this choice of strategies testifies to the accuracy of Cole's sonnet, published earlier in the year of Sheppard's attack.[42]

In "Mesmerism," though, poetic form does more than comment on the depicted sexual violence; it also enacts it. For Campo, the love sonnet form accomplishes idealistic functions. Evoking "the healthy body" and allowing that "the truth be told," it helps the self to heal its painful conflicts. Cole holds a much bleaker view. Fastened to a "choke-chain" of its own design, "Mesmerism" places violent self-loathing at the heart of desire, "the endless dragging of chains that signifies love" (Cole, *Visible Man*, 64). As a love sonnet specifically about gay experience, "Mesmerism" expresses a disturbing ambivalence. Not only does the attacker think of his victim in sexual terms, but the victim finds himself "wanting the face / of the sweaty boy who strangled me." Evoking this idea structurally, victim and attacker share the same poetic form. Certainly the victim does not want a brutal beating, one hastens to add, and of course nothing justifies it. Yet the poem is less interested in these polite, necessary qualifications than showing how degradation fuels desire. "This was not nobility," the first speaker says of himself. Instead, his actions seem closer to genuine pathology, as his lust for his attacker turns violence into a kind of courtship between complementary desires.

Marilyn Hacker registers a potential estrangement from the sonnet tradition by asserting her connection to it much more strongly than Cole and Campo do. While they sprinkle Petrarchan echoes and tropes throughout their sonnets, Hacker saturates *Love, Death, and the Changing of the Seasons* with them. The sequence describes the failed love affair between the speaker and a younger "married" woman, one involved in a same-sex partnership. In addition to its self-consciously Shakespearean plot and its many allusions to his works, this sequence about a failed lesbian love affair begins and ends with Shakespeare's sonnets. The first epigraph is from Sonnet 73, which the sequence's final poem returns to, revising Shakespeare's anguished statement into an anguished question:

> Did you love well what very soon you left?
> Come home and take me in your arms and take
> away this stomach ache, headache, heartache.
> Never so full, I never was bereft
> so utterly. The winter evenings drift
> dark to the window. Not one word will make
> you, where you are, turn in your day, or wake
> from your night toward me. The only gift
> I got to keep or give is what I've cried,
> floodgates let down to mourning for the dead
> chances, for the end of being young,
> for everyone I loved who really died.
> I drank our one year out in brine instead
> of honey from the seasons of your tongue.[43]

This sonnet's most striking formal feature is Hacker's characteristically heavy use of enjambment. While Campo enjambs verb phrases across quatrains, Hacker enjambs various grammatical figures throughout the entire sonnet.[44]

The enjambments follow a general pattern. In nearly every case, the octave's enjambments announce the speaker's physical and mental anguish:

> The winter evenings drift
> dark to the window.

Like the window that becomes a mirror, this enjambment exists to reveal the speaker's emotional state. The enjambed, alliterated, and metrically inverted phrase registers the speaker's surprise as she discovers her emotions projected onto an otherwise peaceful scene. "The winter evenings drift / dark to" — not the more expected "across" — "the window." The enjambment in the lines

> Come home and take me in your arms and take
> away this stomach ache, headache, heartache,

similarly declares the speaker's suffering. She pleads for a full recognition of her own misery. If the former lover were to "[c]ome home and take me in your arms," she would discover, as the reader does after the enjambment, that the anticipated "me" has disappeared into a collection of pains, "this stomach ache, headache, heartache." She is not just "bereft"; she is "bereft / so utterly."

The sestet's enjambments, however, work differently from the octave's. Their relative paucity (only two in six lines, as opposed to six in the first eight lines) signals this shift. While the octave's enjambments act as agents of the speaker's narcissism, the sestet's gesture toward a clearer sense of future possibilities. Line ten's enjambment is particularly significant; the most important moment occurs in the space between lines ten and eleven:

> The only gift
> I got to keep or give is what I've cried,
> floodgates let down to mourning for the dead
> chances, for the end of being young,
> for everyone I loved who really died.

"Much of what happens in strong or hard enjambments," John Hollander notes, "forces a reinterpretation of the position of the syntactic cut at the line break, based upon the discovered *contre-rejet*."[45] While, as the above analysis suggests, all enjambments play off the reader's expectations, the most effective "strong or hard" ones turn the reader's "reinterpretation" into a revelation.

Line ten offers the poem's most aggressive enjambment and its clearest illustration of this principle. The discovered *contre-rejet*, "chances," reveals "dead" to be an adjective, not, as anticipated, a noun. Thus, "chances" marks the depicted mourning as metaphoric instead of literal; the poet is "mourning for the dead / chances," not, say, "the dead / who haunt my days." This thwarting of the reader's expectations is more than a clever poetic feint. Just as it compels the reader to reinterpret the "syntactic cut," the enjambment records the speaker's growing self-awareness that there are fates worse than her own.

In Hollander's terms, it arranges the speaker's gradual reinterpretation of her life's syntax. She faces "the end of being young," not an actual death. The poem quickly reinforces this recognition, mentioning, "everyone I loved who really died." The otherwise superfluous adverb, "really," acts as an exclamation point, emphasizing the point that "real" deaths differ substantially from metaphoric ones. More subtly, the sestet rhymes its only two enjambments, "dead" and "instead," hinting at an essential difference. "[I]nstead" of "dead," the speaker enjoys life's possibilities for renewal.

While the enjambment registers this insight, its grammatical structure highlights the speaker's sorrow. Lines 10–13 modify one preposition, "for." As in the previous list of "this stomach ache, headache, heartache," these lines name three painful conditions, each more intense than the one that precedes it. Their grammatical parallelism stresses the similarity of literal and figurative mourning, of

> mourning for the dead
> chances, for the end of being young,
> for everyone I loved who really died.

The anaphora's cadences exclaim the speaker's grief; at the same time, this rhythm calls attention to the enjambment that interrupts it.

Counterpointing syntax and line structure, the sonnet reinterprets the language of Petrarchan love. In Petrarchan love, "death and life" are conceived as mere "states of mind," not material conditions (Forster, *Icy Fire*, 19). For this reason, a Petrarchan lover deems a casual love affair to be immortal and its end to be no less tragic than an actual death. In contrast, Hacker's enjambment, "dead / chances" returns a cliché to its origins as a metaphor. Stumbling over this phrase, the speaker reminds herself of grief's limits.

In *Celestial Pantomime: Poetic Structures of Transcendence* (1979), Justus George Lawler proposes his theory of "the 'enjambment of transcendence.'"[46] Citing numerous examples, Lawler persuasively shows that the overcoming of limits acts as "one of the most prevalent and one of the most rich contexts of enjambment" (ibid., 75). Lawler further points to "sexual union" as the most common manifestation of this freedom. As in Keats's exemplary enjambment,

> Into her dream he melted, as the rose
> Blendeth its odor with the violet,

the overflowing of one line into another reveals the sexual act's transcendence of human norms (ibid.).

Lawler's account of enjambment describes the octave in Hacker's sonnet. In it, the speaker pleads for a sexual reunion. If love remains the source of her pain, it also offers her potential relief. Following Lawler, one could easily read the enjambments as echoing the speaker's frustrated desire for transcendence, for her lover to

> Come home and take me in your arms and take
> away this stomach ache, headache, heartache.

In the sestet, though, enjambment turns into a mode of interrogation, not transcendence. The tone remains mournful, but, instead of more pleas, the speaker refers to the relationship in the past tense, "I drank our one year . . ." The enjambment of "dead / chances" tells the reader what unlineated prose cannot: that the speaker has begun to question Petrarchan love's self-destructive gestures. The enjambment hesitates over "dead / chances," inspecting it. An act of critical intelligence interrupts a rote catalogue of complaints. In the process, the speaker shows herself to be deeply anguished but, unlike the speaker of Shakespeare's Sonnets, not "past reason."[47]

Most powerfully in its enjambments, the final sonnet of *Love, Death, and the Changing of the Seasons* gestures toward a more mature, reasonable resolution of an unsuccessful romance. "Friendship is one of the major subjects I write about," Hacker explains in an interview: "Especially for lesbians and gays, friends are real family. This hasn't been explored much in writing: intergenerational friendships, friends who turn into lovers, lovers who become friends. It's our real contribution."[48] While the book's final poem expresses a profound sadness, its more balanced perspective looks toward a potential reconciliation, as (in the words of an earlier poem) "lovers . . . become friends," "bar buddies . . . in a few years" (Hacker, *Love*, 11). Absent Shakespeare's vitriolic self-disgust and anger, the sequence suggests a truly novel outcome for a Petrarchan romance: friendship.

Without any obviously self-reflexive statements, Hacker's sonnet offers a brief history of the form. As I have argued, her enjambments inspect her Petrarchan inheritance. At the same time, she traces the sonnet back to its Italian origins, setting Shakespeare's words in a Petrarchan sonnet, the Italian precursor to the English form. When the poem's technique is most "subversive," it is also most "traditional," as Hacker's aggressive enjambments fall easily within this history. Enjambment enjoys a longer and more established precedent in Italian. While Donne's or Herbert's enjambments constitute novelties within the English tradition, Italian readers long understood this technique to convey "the essence of gravità." "[T]his breaking of the lines, as all the masters tell us," Tasso explains, "confers the highest gravity."[49]

Writing of her attraction to metrical forms, Hacker has cited the "tension" they create, "a mental equivalent of those physical states where pleasure approaches pain, or pain, pleasure."[50] This is love poetry's necessary but not sufficient gambit. In places Hacker's sequence campily and ironically appropriates traditional sonnet technique, but it does not settle for these stances. She, like the other sonneteers I have discussed, knows the limits of irony and camp at least partly because her work follows a long body of gay and lesbian literature expert in such poses. Pained and pleasurable, her sonnets bear love's knowledge, its salvations that approach misery, its metaphors literalized and renewed.

FOUR

WHY NOT THE HEROIC COUPLET?

> One of the [English major] requirements was a course
> in the eighteenth century. I hated the very idea of the
> eighteenth century, with all those smug men writing tight
> little couplets and being so dead keen on reason. So I'd
> skipped it.
>
> —Sylvia Plath, *The Bell Jar*

What We Talk About When We Talk
About the Heroic Couplet

Set in the mid-1790s, the years immediately preceding both the Irish
Rebellion and the first edition of *Lyrical Ballads,* Eavan Boland's aptly
titled "The Death of Reason" (1994) depicts the eighteenth century's
fiery passing. Flames overtake a catalogue of the century's gentle arts
and delicate goods, "the curve and pout / of supple dancing and the
couplet rhyming":

> And the dictates of reason and the blended sensibility
> of tact and proportion—yes
> the eighteenth century ends here
> as her hem scorches and the satin
> decoration catches fire. She is burning down.
> As a house might. As a candle will.
> She is ash and tallow. It is over.[1]

Although the poem's closing image is horrific, its rousing syntax, its
clipped, declarative sentences are incantatory and triumphant. The
ballad—not Wordsworth's "emotion recollected in tranquillity" but the
Irish revolutionaries' "flesh-smell of hatred"—prevails over the heroic
couplet, the poetic form that exemplifies and helps perpetuate all these
evils.

Yet, if "[i]t"—meaning, the Augustan Age, "the dictates of reason and the blended sensibility / of tact and proportion"—is "over," why write about it? The answer is that Boland, like many others, perhaps rightly sees the eighteenth century as at the heart of the most serious problems that plague contemporary Western society. To continue to break its forms, then, is to help liberate ourselves from its influence. Since symmetry is fearful, Boland writes "The Death of Reason" in extremely unbalanced free verse. To compose heroic couplets instead would be akin to emulating the Augustans' "dictates of reason," their self-satisfied ignorance of their society's social inequities.

Because he shares many of these familiar assumptions about the eighteenth century and heroic couplet verse, the poet and novelist Stephen Dobyns offers what could be a prose commentary of Boland's poem in his general discussion of poetic form, "Notes on Free Verse." Elaborating upon the differences between metrical and free verse, Dobyns declares, "The character of any historical period is reflected in its art, which is, in fact, a microcosm of that period." He then cites as examples Pope's "Essay on Criticism," Book II, lines 362–73, and Robert Creeley's "I Know a Man":

> The controlled rhythms, the symmetrical form, the logical unfolding of the argument, even the calm and orderly syntax—all reflect Pope's definition of the cosmos: a definition that he shared with the social class and society to which he belonged. Here is a society that believes in a supreme being and the benevolent order of the universe; a society that believes that a person's life is guided by a clear set of principles and virtues. This is the Age of Reason and the major poetic unit of the period, the heroic couplet, is a microcosmic model of that age.
>
> The twentieth century, on the other hand, has been typified by constant disruption and speed both in the physical and metaphysical aspect of people's lives. It has seen extreme violence, uncertainty and the disintegration of the class system. . . . Indeed, the twentieth century, for all of its discoveries, could be called the Age of Unknowing.[2]

As these passages attest, Boland and Dobyns share three main assumptions. First, both believe that the heroic couplet belongs to a more orderly, artistically refined age. "In the Augustan Age," Boland elsewhere notes, "the couplet seemed a micro-model of the age's intentions: closed-in, certain, attractive to the reason, and finally, reassuring to the limits of that elegant world."[3] This view of eighteenth-century literature and culture recalls the wonderfully evocative title of George Saintsbury's 1916 study, *The Peace of the Augustans: A Survey of Eighteenth Century Literature as a Place of Rest and Refreshment.* Second, both Boland and Dobyns submit that contemporary society is too tumultuous for such a rigid poetic form. To write in couplets, then, is at best anachronistic and at worst politically contemptible or morally offensive. Third, neither accepts, or perhaps even considers, the possibility that a verse form can stand in contradiction to the values of the society that produces it or the themes the poem expresses.

Ironically, all three of these assumptions are themselves anachronistic. The historian Roy Porter noted that "recent historians, however, have dynamited this idyll of Georgian harmony. . . . Georgian England was pockmarked with disorder."[4] In support of his claim, Porter convincingly documented scenes of gangland murder, riots, looting, labor strikes, and violent verbal disputes in the streets, in newspapers, and even on pulpits. Indeed, this rethinking of "The Age of Reason" should come as no great surprise to a careful reader of eighteenth-century poetry. Even in examples limited to the high canon, the world of "A Description of a City Shower" and "The Dunciad" reeks of fearful urban squalor, human viciousness, and "CHAOS," the "Universal Darkness [that] buries All."[5] Because the poets lived in such a literally riotous world, their decision to write in heroic couplets suggests that the strict form documents less the values their society lived by than ones they aspired to—or at least aspired to *on occasion.* By doing so, it might have "reassured" and contested the culture's values. Finally, as evidenced by the popularity of "mock" forms, the Augustans, unlike Boland and Dobyns, keenly appreciated the potentially fruitful tension between form and subject, aspiration and reality.

An important work in this rethinking of Augustan poetry is Margaret Anne Doody's *The Daring Muse: Augustan Poetry Reconsidered* (1985). Instead of stressing the reasonableness of Augustan verse, Doody emphasizes its "excitement" and "strangeness" (3). Her discussion of the heroic couplet announces that it is "the enactment of appetite" (232), not uncontested rationality and stability. Consistent with this perspective is her analysis of representative passages from Pope and Rochester: "We can see in these lines that the couplet has offered the poet rich opportunity . . . for variation, display, and change. That is what couplets do. . . . The couplet demands that the poet keep on the move. It gobbles up language at a great rate, and is a most demanding, if satisfying, verse form, . . . not a closed stanzaic pattern, but a flexible framework allowing perpetual activity."[6] Where Dobyns sees fixity, Doody sees flux. Both, however, understand the heroic couplet as a perfectly neat reflection of Augustan values. For them, the form must seem an echo of whatever sense they make of the period. As a consequence, Doody occasionally overstretches her argument, drawing, at times, some fairly unconvincing connections among historical events, her psychological speculations, and prosodic structure.[7] However, even a reader who remains unconvinced by certain of Doody's points cannot deny that her revisionist literary history achieves its self-stated "major purpose to restore the sense of excitement that can come from a reading of Augustan poetry" (Doody, *Daring Muse*, 2). Indeed, *The Daring Muse* provides vivid testimony to eighteenth-century studies' inspiring development over the last twenty-five years, as Augustan poetry has been revealed to be not the too reasonable verse we plow through in anticipation of the Romantics but a brawling, energetic literature that a student might even enjoy.

Only a contrarian hearing Dobyns's lecture would be inspired to try writing couplets; a class with Doody or Dobyns's former colleague, Felicity Nussbaum, coeditor of *The New 18th Century* (1987), however, might stimulate some experimentation. The contrast between Dobyns's views and the general trend of recent eighteenth-century studies points to more than one poet's disagreement with contemporary scholarship. Rather, it highlights the academic divisions between "creative" and "scholarly" work, which inspires members of the same profession to write very different literary histories for different audiences and different purposes.[8] Dobyns's essay "Notes on Free Verse" boasts a daunting one hundred and eighty-five endnotes, none of which refer to a scholarly study of English-language poetry published within the last fifteen years. The list instead abounds with citations of recent poetry collections and criticism by contemporary poets. Such a disparity, unthinkable for a scholarly literary history such as Doody's, is commonplace for "poet's criticism," which operates under an almost wholly different set of professional standards and conventions.

If the contemporary heroic couplet were a character in a fairy tale, she would be the ugly step-sister, ignored by the suitors who rush to her more attractive companions: the villanelle, pantoum, and sestina.

While poets lavish attention on these more complicated forms, the heroic couplet, the mainstay of English verse for two hundred years, works hard to catch a stranger's eye. Contemporary poets find the heroic couplet so unattractive that it merits no entry in the glossary of terms and forms in David Lehman's anthology, *Ecstatic Occasions, Expedient Forms: 85 Leading Contemporary Poets Select and Comment on Their Poems* (1996).[9] A reader who can't identify the heroic couplet won't miss much. Not one of the eighty-five leading poets offers an example of this form. Beyond the anthology, these days all the heroic couplet seems good for is translation, light verse, and, most frequently, parody.

A possible explanation for this neglect is that the contemporary ear finds close repetitions of rhyme to be grating or just plain silly. However, start scanning your FM radio and you will hear an impressive variety of songs written in nonmetrical rhyming pairs. Genres as different as gangsta rap and easy listening, top 40 and punk, R&B and country and western all share a fondness for this form. With a deft rhyme millions of Americans learned in a single day, Johnnie Cochran demonstrated that the rhyming couplet has lost little of its mnemonic power. Indeed, "If the glove doesn't fit, you must acquit" proved to be nothing if not rhetorically persuasive.

Unlike Cochran's and Garth Brooks's rhymes, the heroic couplet adheres to conventional definitions of a "literary" form, a fact that underscores the crucial role that literary history plays in the form's reception. With a sly pun J. M. Coetzee describes a reception for a visiting writer. "My husband is in the eighteenth century," a guest volunteers, hoping to start a conversation. The writer replies:

> "Ah, yes. A good place to be. The Age of Reason."
> "I do not believe we see the period in quite so uncomplicated a way nowadays," says Professor Goodwin. He seems to be about to say more, but then does not.[10]

While the sonnet's recent history confirms that cutting-edge scholarship can inspire poets, the heroic couplet's general neglect amid what some call "revivals of traditional technique"[11] highlights a less productive situation, one marked by condescension and ignorance. Many writers remain unaware of recent scholarship on the heroic couplet and the possibilities it raises; many scholars follow Professor Goodwin's example, unable to speak to the living practitioners of the arts they study. In contrast to queer theory, which entered conversations across disciplines and fields, news of "the new 18th century" has reached few poets. As a consequence even creative writers interested in writing metrical verse seem content to repeat the lessons that John Berryman's professor teaches:

> Let me tell you how
> The Eighteenth Century couplet ended. Now
> Tell me.[12]

Of course the answers the tenured bore looks for are familiar enough to be clichés: Coleridge's "organic form," a few key phrases from the *Lyrical Ballads'* Preface, and Arnold's dismissal of Dryden and Pope as "classics of our prose."

But Is It Poetry?

> Rhymed couplets are unlikely to compete with De
> Maupassant, let alone with Hollywood.
>   If one is convinced that the film offers, in the present
> century, a better form than the stage, he is unlikely to
> advise anyone to write any *more* rhymed couplets.
>   Ezra Pound

"What's next, powdered wigs?" a skeptic might ask. "Even if the heroic couplet worked more interestingly than some of us believe, does it follow that it still works? Isn't Pound right that the time to write heroic couplets has passed and the form is obsolete?"

To answer these questions, I turn to three fairly recent poems in heroic couplets that most subtly challenge our assumptions about that form: Thom Gunn's "Lament," Derek Mahon's "Yaddo Letter," and Derek Walcott's "The Spoiler's Return." Just as the heroic couplet's lengthy history should not be reduced to the single figure of Alexander Pope, the contemporary couplet's surprisingly wide range of possibilities needs to be acknowledged. Like the sonnet during the eighteenth century, the couplet has not been wholly abandoned but exists as an extremely minor form that has nevertheless attracted several distinguished contemporary poets.

Of course another writer would choose other poems to discuss. For example, James Merrill's *The Changing Light at Sandover* might be shown to demonstrate the heroic couplet's continued capacity for urbane wit and playfulness. Also, Marilyn Hacker's wild enjambments and frank discussions of contemporary sexual mores might be said to violate the couplet's rules of formal and aesthetic decorum — but only if one accepts that such rules exist.

Instead of Merrill's or Hacker's verse, I wish to start with Thom Gunn's "Lament." Given such a title, the poem's dispassionate tone might surprise a reader unfamiliar with Gunn's work:

> Your dying was a difficult enterprise.
>
> First, petty things took up your energies,
> The small but clustering duties of the sick,
> Irritant as the cough's dry rhetoric.
> Those hours of waiting for pills, shot, X-ray
> Or test (while you read novels two a day)
> Already with a kind of clumsy stealth
> Distanced you from the habits of your health.[13]

Later, Gunn describes his friend's stoicism during his last days:

> And when at last the whole death was assured,
>
> Drugs having failed, and when you had endured
> Two weeks of an abominable constraint,
> You faced it equably, without complaint,
> Unwhimpering, but not at peace with it.
>   (Ibid., 63)

These couplets depict a friend's death from AIDS but do so with an attitude Boland might call Augustan. For her, "the dictates of reason and the blended sensibility / of tact and proportion" (Boland, *Time of Violence*, 6) should be condemned. "Lament" celebrates these values as noble. Gunn's deft use of the heroic couplet form aspires not to the "perpetual activity" (Doody, *Daring Muse*, 237) to which Doody refers but to a firm, formal control modeled upon his friend's unself-pitying composure as he confronts his own mortality. Just as the patient faces death "without complaint," Gunn elegizes him with couplets whose fiercely restrained tone and versification are similarly "[u]nwhimpering, but not at peace" with the fatal illness. This point can best be seen in the key rhyme of the two passages quoted above:

> The small but clustering duties of the sick,
> Irritant as the cough's dry rhetoric.

To describe a full-blown AIDS patient's painful, sometimes violent, hacking fits as "dry rhetoric" is to offer a trope of startling understatement. However, this rhyme and the sentiment it expresses are wholly appropriate; following the patient's example, the poet offers the rhetorical equivalent of his friend's stoicism: an elegantly, almost austerely unadorned meter, pared-down rhymes, and the plain, discursive style of Winters, Cunningham, and Pinsky.

Expanding upon this idea, the poem's final lines poignantly demonstrate why "Lament" needed to be written in heroic couplets. Set in the speaker's garden the day after his friend's death, "Lament" concludes by meditating upon the relation between life's "variations" and sickness's "inconsistencies":

> I was delivered into time again
>
> —The variations that I live among
> Where your long body too used to belong
> And where the still bush is minutely active.
>   [N]ear the end it [your body] let you down for good,
> Its blood hospitable to those guests who
> Took over by betraying it into
> The greatest of its inconsistencies
> This difficult, tedious, painful enterprise.
>   (Gunn, *Man with Night Sweats*, 64)

As a versification term, "variations" calls the reader's attention to this passage's underlying metaformalism. The need for metrical variation is particularly acute in extended heroic couplet verse such as "Lament" because the proximity of the rhymes to each other, their easily discernible pattern, and the repetitiousness inherent in a longer verse form demand departures from the established metrical pattern.

Gunn above all fears excesses of "variations" or, as he calls them, "inconsistencies," the worst and most grave of which is the body's gradual deterioration into fatal disease. Eliding the metrical with the medical, "Lament" sympathetically portrays a dying man's determined battle to control the rate of change as the couplets engage in an equally dogged pursuit of tonal and prosodic consistency (but not, I hasten to add, monotony). Gunn's rhyme of "who" with "into" links a one-syllable, three-letter pronoun with a two-syllable, four-letter preposition. This is not inconsistent with Augustan practice that rhymes "rows" and "Billet-doux," and "Pope" and "elope" (Pope, *Poems of Alexander Pope*, 222, 598). Yet the linguistic and phonetic variation involved in Gunn's couplet is deliberately and appropriately subdued. In a time of plague, then, the poet, elegizing his friend by following his courageous example, struggles with "[t]his difficult, painful, and tedious enterprise" by appealing to the well-established, formal patterns of life and art.

By doing so, Gunn's couplets raise the broader generic issue of what implications should be seen in his decision to write in a verse form that has lost its privileged cultural standing. One of the very few views of the couplet shared by Dobyns, Doody, and the form's previous generation of scholars is that the closed couplet often functioned, as William Bowman Piper notes in *The Heroic Couplet* (1969), "as a medium for public discourse . . . [which] wonderfully satisfied the vital need of the seventeenth and eighteenth centuries to formulate public statements and to carry on public discussion."[14] Even if Gunn's couplets were to adhere strictly to the Augustan conventions, they still would not function as "a medium for public discourse" because the late-twentieth-century public no longer accepts this form as the proper vehicle to satisfy their civic needs. However, Gunn's couplets do act as an effective rhetorical device to emphasize that this poem is a self-consciously public, not private, elegy about AIDS. Without referring explicitly to any of the controversies that, during the eighties, raged over AIDS-related issues such as the proper level of governmental funding for research, "Lament" carefully details the agonies a dying man endures and the courage he displays without any witnesses except his nurse, his father, and one friend. The couplets underscore the fact that this seemingly private event informs the very public issues of the wretched deaths AIDS patients endured in the 1980s, as they faced inadequate medical options and a culture that largely ignored or trivialized their plight. In the late twentieth and early twenty-first century, the heroic couplet, therefore, may not be a major "medium for public discourse," but it can be effective in acknowledging what and whom the public discourse ignores.

While "Lament" shows the contemporary couplet's ability to address even desperately topical issues, Derek Mahon's "The Yaddo Letter" usefully reminds us that neither history nor the heroic couplet began in the eighteenth century. For the most part, when we talk about the heroic couplet we refer to its use in the eighteenth century, the form's most conspicuous and productive period. But Mahon's couplets recall seventeenth-century country house poems of patronage.[15] In particular, "The Yaddo Letter" brings to mind Thomas Carew's "To My Friend G. N. from Wrest."

As in other country house poems about literary benefactors, Carew praises his patron's wide-ranging generosity:

> at large tables filled with wholesome meats
> The servant, tenant, and kind neighbor eats.
> Some of that rank spun of a finer thread
> Are with the women, Steward, and Chaplain fed
> With daintier cates; others, of better note,
> Whom wealth, parts, office, or the herald's coat
> Have severed from the common, freely sit
> At the Lord's table, whose spread sides admit
> A large access of friends.
>
> (Ibid., 90)

According to this highly idealized portrait, the patron's household is a hierarchy that works, a "house for hospitality" (ibid., 89) whose order is both benevolent and responsible. Although some diners eat "daintier cates" and some more "wholesome meats," all those fortunate enough to gain an invitation enjoy a cordial feast. As opposed to the chaotic outer world, Wrest offers "temperate air" (ibid.), which Carew praises with equally temperate couplets. His gently enjambed lines do not break into grammatically distinct pairs but proceed with an easy formality suggestive of the graceful, well-satisfied movements of the swans and other creatures as they enjoy the estate's ornamental waters. Avoiding harsh notes of bitterness or complaint, the couplets "wander freely where they please / Within the circuit of our narrow seas" (ibid., 91). Instead of singing in their chains like the sea, these couplets contentedly glide forward, delighting in the permissive yet protective order that buoys their wanderings.

Mahon's couplets, like those of Carew, introduce the members of the country household he visits:

> I've a composer in the next-door suite
> called Gloria (*in excelsis*), an English novelist,
> a sculptor from Vermont, a young ceramist
> from Kansas; for we come in suns and snows
> from *everywhere* to write, paint and compose.[16]

As in "To My Friend G. N. from Wrest," these gracefully enjambed couplets employ an elegantly informal, almost conversational style to depict a distinguished country refuge for artists. This household, however, is not an English estate complete with Ladies, Gentlemen, servants, Stewards, Chaplains, and other idealized figures seated according to social rank. Instead, set at Yaddo, an artists' retreat in upstate New York, the poem presents a rather eccentric congregation of artists who come "from *everywhere* to write, paint and compose." The least likely figure is the poet himself, an Irishman writing a verse epistle to his children from a marriage ended in divorce.

Given these obvious differences between "The Yaddo Letter" and "To My Friend G. N. from Wrest," why does Mahon choose to write couplets? Unlike Gunn, he does not primarily seek a sense of formal control; unlike Carew, he does not write couplets whose movement is meant to mirror either the gracefulness of a grand estate's grounds or the easy unpretentiousness of the household. Finally, in contrast to Pope, who wrote heroic couplets almost exclusively, Mahon lives in an age that offers a poet a spectrum of formal options vast and accessible as the nearest copy of *The New Princeton Encyclopedia of Poetry and Poetics*.

By drawing upon the form's historical and literary associations, the heroic couplets of "The Yaddo Letter" set up an implicit comparison between contemporary poetic cultures and those of the past. No essential link exists between the heroic couplet and patronage. However, the large body of significant verse in that form about that subject begs for a generic reading of "The Yaddo Letter," one that takes into account not just individual elements of its versification but the larger backdrop of heroic couplet poems about patronage and the literary and historical situations they represent.

With great precision "The Yaddo Letter" details the institutions behind Mahon's subsidized wanderings; he travels to Yaddo in upstate New York in order to compose poetry for a reading sponsored by the 92nd Street Y before returning home to Dublin. In patronage's latest renaissance, then, the poets come calling to America, not courtly England. Flush with money, the former colony's institutions—not old-world aristocrats, book subscribers, or the general reading public—are the poet's new best friends. Indeed, as America imports whom it judges to be the other English-speaking nations' finest poets, it is not surprising that some of the most notable Irish poems are being written in America, by, among others, Mahon, Boland, Seamus Heaney, and Paul Muldoon. As the title proclaims, Mahon writes "The Yaddo"—not the Wrest, the Twickenham or the O'Connell Street—"Letter." Evoking other heroic couplet poems about patronage as points of comparison and departure, Mahon's verse reminds us that under late capitalism Culture is Taste with charismatic fundraisers and not-for-profit status.

Given Mahon's purposes, heroic couplets help him to situate his poem as fully as possible in the social, historical, and literary issues of patronage, America's cultural and financial dominance, and poetry's increasing institutionalization and marginalization. In "The Yaddo Letter," heroic couplets do not offer Mahon a dangerously nostalgic, politically naive or reactionary escape from history. Rather, they provide the most effective formal instruments for a deeply considered dialogue between the individual and culture, poet and international power, and the present and past.

The couplets of "The Yaddo Letter" record even the forces they resist. In particular, "The Yaddo Letter" features highly conversational, heavily enjambed couplets whose versification conspires to make the rhymes and, thus, the verse form less grating to an ear accustomed to free verse. As I have argued, these couplets recall Carew's; at the same time, Mahon is a contemporary, not a Renaissance, poet, and, living in an age that so disfavors this particular verse form, he composes pairs of lines which whisper, not declaim, that they are heroic couplets.

To call verse such as Mahon's traditional does not get us very far, as all poetry, even the most self-consciously avant-garde, appeals to some tradition—or, more precisely, traditions. Instead, the more pressing concern is which traditions the new poem claims. Of all the contemporary poets who write rhymed, metrical verse, the one whose work shows the greatest appreciation of this truth is Derek Walcott.

As Walcott argues in "North and South," this lesson was lost on nearly an entire generation of American poets. Living in America, the middle-aged Walcott is startled by the abundance of poetry that offers little more than advertisements for itself:

> and these days in bookstores I stand paralyzed
> by the rows of shelves along whose wooden branches
> the free-verse nightingales are trilling "Read me! Read Me!"
> in various metres of asthmatic pain.[17]

These "free-verse nightingales" are firm believers in what James Longenbach terms "the 'breakthrough' narrative."[18] As Longenbach persuasively argues, too many critics and poets not only uncritically accepted Lowell's characterization of *Life Studies* (1959) as "a breakthrough back into life" but applied that elegantly evasive phrase as a litmus test for contemporary poetry. "[F]or many years a poet's prestige depended on the strength of his or her 'breakthrough'" (ibid.), Longenbach astutely notes. By general consensus, free verse was deemed not just the only "authentic" verse form but an effective prescription for "psychic and political health" (ibid.).

In "North and South," Walcott sharpens Longenbach's critique. In particular, Walcott perceives a generation's collective decision to write only in free verse as a "breakthrough" to poetic narcissism, not life. Limited to this single form and to the single subject of the writer's melodramatic distress, the resulting poems are nearly indistinguishable to Walcott. "Read me! Read me!" the poets trill in "various metres of asthmatic pain," saying the same thing in almost exactly the same way. According to "North and South," these late confessional poets present their hypochondriac ailments as life-or-death matters, writing out of unchecked self-regard because they literally do not know any better.

Given Walcott's rather extreme views and often satiric vision, it is not surprising that he has tried writing in the unfashionable heroic couplet form. "The Spoiler's Return," an extended poem in couplets, ends:

Catch us in Satan tent, next carnival:
Lord Rochester, Quevedo, Juvenal,
Maestro, Martial, Pope, Dryden, Swift, Lord Byron,
the lords of irony, the Duke of Iron,
hotly contending for the monarchy
in couplets or the old re-minor key,
all those who gave earth's pompous carnival
fatigue, and groaned "O God, I feel to fall!"
all those whose anger for the poor on earth
made them weep with a laughter beyond mirth,
names wide as oceans when compared with mine
salted my songs, and gave me their high sign.
All you excuse me, Spoiler was in town;
you pass him straight, so now he gone back down.
                            (Walcott, *Collected Poems*, 438)

The fact that "The Spoiler's Return" seems to break so many of Pope's metrical principles affirms that a poetic form is a set of organizing principles arranged and rearranged according to historic and artistic necessity, not a list of transhistorical rules. In order to understand the formal principles of "The Spoiler's Return," then, I will set the poem in three overlapping contexts, relating it to its formal precedents, contemporary English-language poetry, and the highly politicized situation of the Afro-Caribbean artist.

"The Spoiler's Return" dramatizes the paradoxical challenges any contemporary poet faces when writing in a form so rich in history as the heroic couplet. More precisely, Walcott carefully details how a formal homage evolves into challenge, then into a more intense homage between equals, or what Eliot calls "a deeper communion."[19] In fact, poetic form provides the very medium for this complex exchange. In the first third of the poem, Spoiler appreciatively quotes the opening six lines of Rochester's "A Satire Against Mankind." As this act of homage attests, Walcott's satiric, sometimes crassly idiomatic and anatomical couplets deliberately imitate Rochester's similar handling of the form. The heroic couplet, then, offers Walcott the formal device with which to direct another satire against mankind, and, in the process, to express his reverence for his literary ancestors. Indeed, Walcott shows how, like a litany of saints, their very names are poetry. However, by writing couplets that "cackle with a language beyond mirth," the poet claims his right to challenge the others for "the monarchy of couplets." In this respect, his verse—and versification—stage a determined power-play. Although Harold Bloom, still the most prominent contemporary critic of poetic influence, might see in this interaction "the dark truths of competition and contamination"[20] involved in a poet's development, Walcott depicts a gentler process closer to Eliot's vision in which "the *whole* existing order must be, if ever so slightly, altered."[21] Ultimately, the poet works together with his predecessors, honoring them and honored by them. As Spoiler brags in his final reference to the other poets, they "salted my songs, and gave me their high sign." By writing couplets, Walcott revises their conventions but, in the process, argues for this currently unpopular form's contemporary relevance. To put this idea in terms closer to the poem's, in an act of mutual respect Spoiler teaches the forms of the dead how to sing to the living.

Read in the broad context of late-twentieth-century English-language poetry, the couplets rebuke "the free-verse nightingales" who possess neither the technical skill nor the inclination to learn this demanding form. "The Spoiler's Return" scolds them with its impressively vast technical range. Indeed, "The Spoiler's Return" is both more "literary" and "common" than the short, plainspoken free verse. Walcott's patois is coarser than the language employed by poets who aspire to the appearance of sincerity, yet his worshipful catalogue of several decidedly unfashionable writers is a more self-consciously bookish technique than even the most "academic" poets use.

An earlier passage openly exhibits the poem's imposing formal range:

> [I]t has been done before, all Power has
> made the sky shit and maggots of the stars,
> over these Romans lying on their backs,
> the hookers swaying their enormous sacks,
> until all language stinks, and the truth lies,
> a mass for maggots and a fête for flies;
> and, for a spineless thing, rumour can twist
> into a style the local journalist—
> as bland as a green coconut, his manner
> routinely tart. . . .
>
> (Walcott, *Collected Poems*, 435)

This passage deftly contrasts its own style with that of the journalist, whose blandness, "spineless" conformity, and predictably unmodulated tone evokes Walcott's similar dismissal of "the free-verse nightingales" in "North and South." In derision, Walcott flaunts prosodic and tonal effects too numerous to catalogue except partially. The opening line is abstract and broadly historical, and thus appears greatly detached from the historical processes it describes. In a startling contrast, the second line offers a vision both scatological and metaphoric. Yet, by so relishing the nastiness of its details, the next couplet plainly recalls similar verses of Rochester, one of the members of Spoiler's chorus. The third couplet works in a manner similar to the first, as the abstract statement about history precedes the scatological and metaphoric vision. Yet, while the metaphors' tenors are very similar—"shit" and "flies," "maggots" and "maggots"—their vehicles are remarkably different. Instead of celestial imagery made excretory, the third couplet introduces a horror of language's debasement with the mixed metaphors of a rancid religious ceremony and a carnival celebration. By the time a reader reaches the first reference to the journalist as "a spineless thing," the message is unmistakably clear. "[B]land as a green coconut," the unripened style of both journalism and, by implication, other poetry sadly pales in comparison to Walcott's overpowering formal exuberance.

The differences between "The Spoiler's Return" and the poetry it implicitly condemns are far greater than those indicated by the rather crude categories of free and metrical verse, or even between free verse and heroic couplets. About the time Walcott wrote "The Spoiler's Return," Robert Hass published a much-noticed lament: "It does seem to be the case that the power of free verse has had something to do with its revolt against some alternative formal principle that feels fictitious. That was certainly part of the excitement of first reading Creeley and Ginsberg, Duncan and Dorn. . . . Now, I think, free verse has lost its edge, become neutral, the given instrument."[22] Hass's observation is helpful yet overly broad. By the mid-eighties, careful readers of contemporary poetry could not help but notice that a particular, highly formulaic kind of "free verse"—not free verse in general—had become the norm. Derided by a diverse assortment of poets and critics with insults ranging from "emaciated poetry," "the scenic mode," "the McPoem," "the flat style," and, most commonly, "the workshop poem,"[23] this kind of free verse is characterized not just by an absence of rhyme and meter, but also, as Marjorie Perloff notes, "the 'I-as-sensitive-register,' the 'direct' colloquial diction . . . the enjambed free-verse line, the 'flat' description . . . and, most important, the Romantic faith in the power of ordinary, everyday experience to yield 'thoughts that do often lie too deep for tears'" (Perloff, *Poetic License*, 63). To revise Hass's complaint, this inventory of formal conventions is "the given instrument" of much verse writing from the sixties to the present.

This background helps us to see that Walcott's particular kind of heroic couplet sets his verse in direct contrast to a particular kind of free verse. He writes in a range of prosodic, linguistic, and stylistic effects far beyond the narrow confines of the prevalent poetry. As a consequence, the luxurious resources of Walcott's couplets show more clearly than any polemic the desperately impoverished condition of this specific free verse.

When seen in the more immediate context of the Caribbean, Walcott's couplets register his fierce refusal to accept the forms and, thus, the cultural and artistic identities others loudly assign to him. In his introduction to *'Dream on Monkey Mountain' and Other Plays* (1970), Walcott offers a searching critique of the artistic and cultural pressures exerted on what he calls "Afro-Christian" artists. After describing two kinds of writers—one who chooses "the language of the people" and the other who chooses "English"—Walcott praises a third type "dedicated to purifying the language of the tribe, and it is he who is jumped on by both sides for pretentiousness or playing white. He is the mulatto of style. The traitor. The assimilator."[24] In this context, writers choose a language and artistic forms that are either Eurocentric or Afrocentric. The first writer might compose couplets in the Queen's English, the second sea chanteys in "the language of the people." In contrast, Walcott patterns himself after the most widely attacked artist, "the mulatto of style" who makes use of formal options as complex as his cultural situation, writing a sea chantey in the Queen's English and heroic couplets in patois.

Expanding on this idea, Walcott argues, "Pastoralists of the African revival should know that what is needed is not new names for old things, or old names for old things, but the faith of using the old names anew" (ibid., 10). Indeed, "The Spoiler's Return" literalizes this metaphor, using "anew" the "old names" of

Lord Rochester, Quevedo, Juvenal,
Maestro, Martial, Pope, Dryden, Swift, Lord Byron.

These are the heroes of the classical, colonial education Walcott received at St. Mary's College in Castries and the University of West Indies in Jamaica. However, even if one does not accept Walcott's belief that Calypso is "pentametric in composition,"[25] it is incontrovertible that his couplets set these figures in an almost wholly unexpected context. Just as "Juvenal" is shown to rhyme with "carnival," the poem's Calypso-influenced rhythms and Caribbean vernacular pronounce in a creole accent some of the English canon's loftiest names. Borrowing Calypso conventions from the Mighty Spoiler, Theophilus Phillip, a former Calypso Monarch of Carnival,[26] "The Spoiler's Return" shows how Eurocentric and Caribbean traditions are, at times, literally indistinguishable. Quoting Rochester's "A Satire Against Mankind," the poem simultaneously calls to mind the Mighty Spoiler's "Bedbug," which starts with a paraphrase of Rochester's lines. The result is a Calypso heroic couplet, a carnival of old and new worlds, of forms descended from slave songs and from classical European verse. The "faith," then, that Walcott professes is a steadfast conviction not to whittle from his poetry nor its forms the lessons either of the street or the classroom.

Walcott's messy couplets allude to Pope and Rochester, but Augustan verse simply cannot account for his usages. Indeed, with their elegant balance of humility and arrogance, erudition and earthiness, "The Spoiler's Return" demonstrates the transnational, transcultural nature of poetic form. A particular verse form might work better for a certain time and place than for others; however, Walcott's deft use of the Calypso couplet warns its readers not to assign to any poetic form a stable cultural, aesthetic, or artistic value. Instead, as "The Spoiler's Return" confirms, in order to understand the forms poets favor, it is necessary to understand those they neglect. For this reason, even though contemporary poets generally ignore the heroic couplet, critics of contemporary poetry should not, if only to release both "the free-verse nightingales" and the new formalists from equally narrow ranges of formal possibility.

FIVE

ON THE CONTEMPORARY BALLAD

IN 1972 DOROTHY AND X. J. KENNEDY FOUNDED AN IMPROBABLE JOURNAL.
In a period dominated by free verse, *Counter / Measures: A Magazine of Rime, Meter and Song* published only poetry that used those unfashionable techniques. A quintessential small magazine, it failed to achieve a wide circulation. (It did receive a remarkable number of submissions: more than 3,700.)[1] After the third and final issue, subscribers with unfulfilled balances received refund checks. For nearly three decades unsold back issues languished in the Kennedys' garage until the editors finally carted them to the town dump.

Short lived and largely forgotten, *Counter / Measures* remains more than a historical curiosity. It published the early work of many poets who, in the late 1980s, would spearhead the new formalist movement, such as Timothy Steele, Gjertrud Schnackenberg, and Charles Martin. It mixed these new voices with well-established figures of midcentury metrical verse, including Anthony Hecht, J. V. Cunningham, and Richard Wilbur. It did so in a spirit at odds with much discussion of verse technique. "[P]lease believe," the editors implored, "that in confining this magazine to poetry that embodies meter and/or rime, we have nothing against poetry that doesn't. We try merely to question the rumor that meter and rime are no more."[2] This passage's judicious tone remains striking. A rather technical, seemingly unemotional subject, prosody generates vitriolic debates, *ad hominen* attacks, and politically charged polemics. A poet's choice of verse form inspires partisan rancor because the poetic culture reads it as a gesture of group allegiance. A Petrarchan sonnet marks its author as "a formalist" while a sequence that employs Oulipian composition methods establishes another poet's avant-gardist credentials. In contrast *Counter / Measures* welcomed poets of very different artistic lineages and interests. In its own words, it sought the work of "names and newcomers, including a few you wouldn't expect to catch dead in a place like this."[3] Certainly it is the only magazine to publish Hecht, Cunningham, and Wilbur alongside song lyrics by Louis and Celia Zukofsky, Sonny Boy Williamson, Lightnin' Hopkins, and Keith and Rosmarie Waldrop.

As its subtitle suggests, *Counter / Measures* published blues and ballads because it promoted the connections between *"Rime, Meter and Song."* In order to advocate what the poet and anthologist Robert Richman calls a "return to musicality," new formalist criticism often claims that meter possesses a superior musicality to free verse. Richman, for instance, posits that "a recent upsurge among poets in the use of metrical language" raises "[t]he sheer sensuous appeal of the verse."[4] *Counter / Measures* proposes a stricter yet more nuanced understanding of the relation between poetry and song. Instead of pursuing vague analogies between metrical and musical technique, the editors sought "to encourage poets to write more songs—real songs, the kind with tunes to them."[5] These "real songs" included blues lyrics and traditional and literary ballads, sources from "high" and "low" cultures. The journal's first frontispiece quoted Allen Ginsberg, "I hear ghostly Academics in Limbo screeching about Form." The poems that appeared inside the next issue, though, suggested that the very bluesman Ginsberg venerated employed the metrical techniques he disparaged, "meter and/or rime." Instead, the journal's emphasis on song served a strong reminder that meter inspires all kinds of lyrics, not just pedantry.[6]

The journal printed sheet music for some lyrics. Others featured insistent rhythms that invited the reader to discover the "tune." Consider the opening stanza of Rosmarie Waldrop's "I Can't Keep up with You":

> I have a neat pair of scissors
> you have a switchblade knife
> when I kissed my first man

you divorced your second wife
I can't keep up with you.[7]

A reader who silently mouths these words fails to experience them fully. Instead, he or she must perform them, interpret the written document as a script for verbal articulation. Nicely characterizing this process, Langston Hughes once introduced his work as "Blues, ballads, and reels to be read aloud, crooned, shouted, recited, and sung. Some with gestures, some not—as you like. None with a far-away voice."[8] Indeed, "a far-away voice," the dreamy "poet's voice" that contemporary writers affect for public readings, would comically mangle Waldrop's ballad. Instead, it demands a more robust articulation, one that considers how the printed text invites its readers to read it aloud, croon, shout, recite, and sing.

Counter / Measures's catholicity reminds us how few accounts do justice to metrical verse's rich, complex achievement. For instance, racial segregation governs most discussions of poetic form. By any definition, the ballad is a "traditional" form. Yet many studies of "traditional" prosody fail to mention Hughes, Gwendolyn Brooks, or any other African American masters; more shockingly, some "general" studies of the ballad in English unselfconsciously examine only white poets' work.[9] Redrawing the racial, philosophical, and critical boundaries that literary history constructs, the ballad attracts poets of different races and temperaments because it offers them a resource to address contemporary poetry's most pressing challenge. For at least two decades the confessional lyric has shown to be exhausted. In response contemporary poets have struggled to develop other modes of expression, to reconfigure the relationship between artistic form, the self, and society. Though it has not achieved a notable increase in popularity, the ballad demands attention because it suggests possible solutions, strategies to address the difficulties that lyric poetry currently faces.

In his groundbreaking book, *The Tuning of the World* (1980), R. Murray Schafer coined the term "soundscape" to describe "[t]he sonic environment," the sounds that the inhabitants encounter in particular places and times. Schafer challenged scholars to consider "the relationship between man and the sounds of his environment and what happens when those sounds change." Decades before interdisciplinary work grew routine, Schafer proposed "soundscape studies" as "the middle ground between science, society, and the arts."[10] Responding to Schafer's provocation, more recent scholarship has pursued the fascinating question of how Victorian and Modernist sounds shaped the periods' literature and culture.[11]

But what sounds characterize the contemporary soundscape? Car radios and portable stereos reverberate rhymes through the streets, and televisions carry them into kitchens and bedrooms. Rappers employ a prosody both literally daring and inviting; their rhymes dare poetic rivals to match their technical skills and invite the audience's active participation. When a rapper extends the microphone toward the audience and cups his ear or when she offers the stock invitation

> Throw your hands in the air
> Like you just don't care

the audience's silence constitutes the gravest rejection. The rapper's self-described "rhymes" exist not on the page but in the dynamic between performer and audience. This kind of virtuoso performance differs from those of the "guitar gods" familiar to the 1960s and 1970s, not just because one entertainment remains primarily verbal and the other primarily instrumental. Rappers "represent"; they celebrate their local roots, whether in Compton, Long Beach, or the Bronx; even when they brag of the success they have achieved, their "rhymes" connect performer and audience. Listening to a rap CD, a fan starts to rap.

My point is not that rappers have directly influenced print-based poets. In a few cases they have, although as Tracie Morris laments, their influence remains intragenerational.[12] Rather, at a time when critics routinely dismiss rhyming verse as aesthetically reactionary and "elitist," the contemporary soundscape suggests rhyme's potential to reconfigure the relationship between text and reader, poet and audience. It invites us to rethink what we "know" about the long-established rhyming prosodies we encounter and the effects they currently achieve.

This reconsideration must start with the issue of performance. Poetry scholars generally agree that poetry must be read aloud. Derek Attridge, for instance, sensibly emphasizes the need for a reader to experience a poem's "rhythm," which he defines as "its movement through time." Poetry, he writes, "should be read aloud whenever possible, and even when read silently it should take up the same amount of time that reading aloud would give it."[13] Cognitive science and physiological psychology extend Attridge's point, suggesting that a certain dynamic occurs when a reader chants or sings the words, not just reads them aloud. As Mark W. Booth has argued, singers employ different parts of their brain than speakers do when engaged in conversation. The brain's left hemisphere controls speech function, while the right controls song function. For this reason, patients "who have suffered cerebral hemorrhages on the left hemisphere such that they cannot speak can still sing." In a startling case, a speechless patient sang "America" and "Home on the Range."[14]

Many aspects of brain function remain mysterious even to specialists in the field, a fact that cautions against the wholesale acceptance of "right" and "left" brain function schemes.[15] Still, these preliminary findings hint at the complications that arise when a reader such as Keats, who "chanted" Chatterton's poetry, took print-based words and converted them into the songlike rhythms.[16] We often take for granted the ability to perform such an apparently simple act, but it demands a remarkable level of engagement, of brain activity and participation. Consider the various cognitive functions that occur when a reader follows X. J. Kennedy's instructions and sings his ballad, "In a Prominent Bar in Secaucus One Day," to the tune of "The Old Orange Flute" or "Sweet Betsy from Pike":

> In a car like the Roxy I'd roll to the track,
> A steel-guitar trio, a bar in the back,
> And the wheels made no noise, they turned over so fast,
> Still it took you ten minutes to see me go past.[17]

Interestingly, the poem's tune came as "a surprise," suggested by a friend after he read the completed poem. Kennedy delightedly accepted the recommendation, later remembering, "Ever since then, I have been hoping to write more songs, fewer poems that are merely one-way conversations."[18] Indeed, the multifold "conversation" that occurs when one performs "In a Prominent Bar," involves more than reader and text. Singing these words frustrates our customary reading procedures. A reader who performs the ballad according to the author's instructions encounters techniques that preliterate cultures developed for oral transmission and that contemporary poets have largely abandoned. As Booth writes of the broadside ballad, a print-based ballad offers "a great meeting ground of orality and literacy . . . a long intermediate stage of mental accommodation" (Booth, *Experience of Songs*, 113). Unlike most contemporary poems, it does not imitate speech rhythms: instead, it sets speech to an aggressive, galloping meter. A reader negotiates these differences with every inflection, pause, and held syllable, as he or she recalls the borrowed tune and converts a print-based poem into song lyrics.

Written for the page yet crafted for performance, the literary ballad has long explored the connections between written and oral methods of transmission. It developed from an oral tradition—or, to be more precise, an oral tradition that many authors studied in written form. Thomas Percy's anthology of medieval ballads, *Reliques of Ancient English Poetry* (1765), inspired a romantic revival. Like F. J. Child's ten-volume *The English and Scottish Popular Ballads* (1882–1898), it quickly exerted a profound influence, as Wordsworth acknowledged in 1815: "I do not think there is an able writer in verse of the present day who would not be proud to acknowledge his obligations to the *Reliques*."[19] These poets reworked the ballad's conventions. To speak in general terms, the folk ballad considered impersonal, communal concerns; it featured a formulaic phrasing and rhymes and many repetitions. Its fast-paced narratives presented moments of great intensity, "lingering and leaping," as ballad scholars call this technique. In addition to their other virtues, such features made the poems easier to memorize. Poets such as Wordsworth and Coleridge admired what Percy called the ballad's "pleasing simplicity," but added a modern literary self-consciousness,[20] including a greater emphasis on linguistic inventiveness.

The form's prosody also changed. T. V. F. Brogan notes that "the nature of b[allad] m[eter]" remains "the subject of much dispute" as scholars debate whether the meter should be classified as accentual syllabic or accentual.[21] This lack of scholarly consensus notwithstanding, it seems safe to generalize that literary ballads tend to feature stricter structures than folk ballads. Typically literary ballads employ quatrains (sometimes with added refrains). The first and third lines rhyme. Many variations exist, including the ballad or hymn meter. Arising from the popular ballads and the Protestant hymnals, hymn meters include the long measure (4–4–4–4) and the common meter (4–3–4–3).

Even while undergoing these changes, the ballad never left its roots in oral literature. In this respect, it differs from nearly all other of

Western culture's older verse forms, which more aggressively developed away from their origins in song. Few, if any, contemporary poets write sonnets—"little songs"—for musical performance. In India a thriving musical tradition still exists for the ghazal, but when Western poets took up the form, they abandoned its musical dimension, focusing instead on the form's themes or formal properties.

The ballad continues to emphasize exuberant verbal performance, a fact that distinguishes it from the other meters that print-based poets favor, including iambic pentameter, still English language's most popular meter. Capable of a remarkable range of effects, iambic pentameter attracts many contemporary poets because it helps them to accomplish a familiar task: to imitate the rhythms of speech and quiet meditation, to write poems in the "far-away voice" that Hughes belittles. Ballads impose a much more aggressive metrical base. In a provocative argument, Antony Easthope argues that the Renaissance courtly lyric's displacement of the feudal ballad marks a crucial shift: "The two forms— ballad and the Renaissance courtly poem—exemplify opposed kinds of discourse: one collective, popular, intersubjective, accepting the text as a poem to be performed; the other individualist, elitist, privatized, offering the text as representation of a voice speaking."[22] Easthope's overly schematic argument presents neatly contrasting pairs. English literary history forms a battle between the ballad and the pentameter, with the ballad as the valiant loser. Yet even if one does not accept his characterization of the pentameter as "elitist," Easthope helpfully clarifies how the ballad's performative rhythms create a communal form, or as he calls it, a "collective, popular, intersubjective" discourse. In simpler terms, the ballad demands the reader's active participation, as he or she must articulate its aggressive rhythms.

This reconstitution of the relationship between reader and text partially explains why the ballad appealed to politically minded poets of various allegiances, even during periods that largely rejected metrical verse technique on political grounds. Throughout the twentieth century, the ballad remained a canonical form of African American literature, providing a number of the culture's foundational myths. "No one writes the songs, no one remembers," laments Colson Whitehead's *John Henry Days* (2001).[23] Yet the nearly four-hundred-page novel relentlessly investigates the John Henry myth, "adding verses" to the ballad, as the last chapter's title announces. Indeed, few major statements of

African American aesthetics fail to consider music's influence or the concerns that drive the literary ballad: the connections between "folk" and "literary" traditions, and "collective" and "individual" modes of expression.

One year before the first issue of *Counter / Measures*, Dudley Randall published his anthology, *The Black Poets*. While the editors of *Counter / Measures* understood that American poets largely neglected metrical verse technique, Randall organized *The Black Poets* to show how ballads and folk songs stood at the center of the tradition it presented. Split into two sections, one for "folk poetry," the other for "literary poetry," *The Black Poets* first presented a generous selection of ballads and folk songs because, as Randall's introduction explained, such work constituted "the root and inspiration of later, literary poetry."[24]

In addition to the examples he noted, such as Melvin's B. Tolson's "The Birth of John Henry" and Robert Hayden's "The Ballad of Nat Turner," Randall might have had in mind his own poem, "Ballad of Birmingham." An elegy for one of the four girls killed in the 1963 bombing of Birmingham's Sixteenth Street Baptist Church, the poem tells a bitterly ironic story. To protect her young daughter from possible harm, a mother forbids her from participating in the Freedom March, sending her insead to church to "sing in the children's choir." When she hears the explosion, the mother runs "through the streets of Birmingham / calling for her child":

> She clawed through bits of glass and brick,
> then lifted out a shoe.
> "O, here's the shoe my baby wore,
> but, baby, where are you?"
> (Randall, *Black Poets*, 144)

Like the anonymous speaker, the mother and child are not named because, as in many ballads, the characters remain largely symbolic. Instead, the poem addresses a community in distress. The poem's final question, "baby, where are you?" literalizes this dynamic. The line's different interpretations underscore the poem's aspiration to speak for, and to, the race. Most literally, it expresses the mother's anguish because she cannot find her daughter's remains. It also offers a biting rhetorical challenge, a direct address to the black community, accusing its members of lacking the young girl's courage, her principled willingness to risk injury. She died grotesquely for the cause, "but, baby, where are you?"

The ballad form allows the poem to accomplish contradictory tasks: to honor the community's grief, admonish the cowardly, and urge future action. Placing the poem within the community it admonishes, the verse form suggests that the poem continues the girl's work. Tellingly, "Ballad of Birmingham" employs the very meter of the church hymns the girl performed the day she died: the common meter. By printing the poem as a broadside, Randall also emphasized how the poem belongs to and extends the eighteenth-century elegiac broadside tradition. As James D. Sullivan notes, such poetry "used death as a public occasion for defining the values of the community. The dead provided a moral lesson—either an example of a good Christian death or a warning to sinners."[25] "Ballad of Birmingham" provides both kinds of moral lessons; the girl's "good Christian death" serves as an example to the survivors and a warning that racism leaves no place safe, not even a church. The six grieving figures who adorn the broadside are appropriately faceless, illustrating the ballad's intent to express the community's grief, rather than an individual's.

The 1996 anthology *Rebel Angels: 25 Poets of the New Formalism* includes an instructive pair of ballads: Dana Gioia's "Summer Storm" and Marilyn Nelson's "The Ballad of Aunt Geneva." Of the two poems, Gioia's "Summer Storm" loses less of its resonance when read as a separate lyric because, unlike "The Ballad of Aunt Geneva," it does not form part of a sequence. The poem remembers a wedding reception, where the male speaker shared a brief moment with an attractive stranger:

> I watched you merge into the group,
> Aloof and yet polite.
> We didn't speak another word
> Except to say goodnight.
>
> Why does that evening's memory
> Return with this night's storm—
> A party twenty years ago,
> Its disappointments warm?

> There are so many *might have beens*,
> *What ifs* that won't stay buried,
> Other cities, other jobs,
> Strangers we might have married.
>
> And memory insists on pining
> For places it never went,
> As if life would be happier
> Just by being different.[26]

"Summer Storm" expresses Gioia's most familiar theme, regret, which, not coincidentally, constitutes one of the most private emotions. As in "Summer Storm," regret creates an internal dialogue between the hypothetical and the realized: the life that "might have [been]" and the life that developed. It would be cruelly tactless for the married speaker to tell his wife what he has been thinking, to share his reverie about the "[s]trangers" he might have married. Like the woman he remembers, he remains "[a]loof and yet polite." Crucially absent, she remains the poem's putative audience, the pretense for its second-person address. Of course the poem does not communicate with her but with the speaker's projection of her. "Summer Storm" does what Romantic theory argues poetry should do: present "feeling"—or, as Gioia calls it, "memory"— "confessing itself to itself."[27]

The ballad structure completes this project, sealing the private self from the outside world. The poem shifts from a party scene, a "rented patio," to an increasingly private interior landscape. Instead of poetic characters, abstractions such as "might have beens," "[w]hat ifs," and "memory" inhabit this depopulated psychic terrain. Similarly, the poem enforces a kind of reticence, a metrical frame between itself and the experience it discusses. Consider the poem's end:

> And memory insists on pining
> For places it never went,
> As if life would be happier
> Just by being different.

Like the rest of "Summer Storm," this stanza mutes the ballad's exuberant rhythms until it approaches the "far-away voice" that Hughes disparaged. The language remains "poetic," with rhymes such as "never went" and "different" that counterpoint spoken language's usual inflections. While this formality distinguishes "Summer Storm" from nonpoetic discourse, the poem's dulled rhythms never reach the ballad's typical intensity, its invitation to song. Matching rhythm to theme, the poem domesticizes the traditional ballad's pining over lost love. The speaker meets his *"belle dame sans merci"* at a wedding reception, where social connections smooth their introductions:

> You knew the groom from college.
> I was a friend of the bride.

R. S. Gwynn's affectionate parody, "Dana Gioia," clarifies how this poem's quotidian details approach the banal:

> Perhaps we should have gone elsewhere
> For carnal intercourse.
> Later we might have been married,
> Had some kids, got a divorce.[28]

The parody's comic boorishness gently mocks the original's good manners. "Summer Storm" relies upon tact and reticence, its "[a]loof and yet polite" rhythms and sensitively reserved persona. It resists the ballad's freewheeling traditions, its roots in earthy folk literature. Though the poem must be classified as a ballad, it largely eschews the resources that the form offers. A lack of bad taste enervates the poem; it produces a wistful, soft-spoken lyricism familiar to much contemporary poetry, metrical or not. Instead of employing heightened rhythms for expressive purposes, the lyric speaks like the two almost-lovers "in whispers" (Gioia, *Interrogations at Noon*, 66).

Rebel Angels also includes a strikingly different ballad: Marilyn Nelson's "The Ballad of Aunt Geneva." "The Ballad of Aunt Geneva" first appeared in Nelson's *The Homeplace* (1989), a book-length sequence that traces the author's ancestry, starting with her great-great-grandmother, a slave. As in Rita Dove's *Thomas and Beulah: Poems* (1986) and Natasha Trethewey's more recent collection, *Domestic Work: Poems* (2000), the poem's familial knowledge also advances the larger project of recovering African American cultural history, what the book calls the "generations lost to be found."[29]

"The Ballad of Aunt Geneva" considers the poet's most notorious ancestor, her great-aunt. Borrowing a technique from folk ballads, it begins and ends with the same quatrain:

> Geneva was the wild one.
> Geneva was a tart.
> Geneva met a blue-eyed boy
> and gave away her heart.

The rest of the poem elaborates on Geneva's disreputable life. To give a sense of Nelson's method, it is necessary to quote the poem in some length:

> They say she killed a woman
> over a good black man
> by braining the jealous heifer
> with an iron frying pan.
>
> They say, when she was eighty,
> she got up late at night
> and sneaked her old, white lover in
> to make love, and to fight.
>
> First, they heard the tell-tale
> singing of the springs,
> then Geneva's voice rang out:
> *I need to buy some things,*
>
> *So next time, bring more money.*
> *And bring some moxie, too.*
> *I ain't got no time to waste*
> *on limp white mens like you.*
>
> *Oh yeah? Well, Mister White Man,*
> *it sure might be stone-white,*
> *but my thing's white as it is.*
> *And you know damn well I'm right.*
>
> *Now listen: take your heart pills*
> *and pay the doctor mind.*
> *If you up and die on me,*
> *I'll whip your white behind.*

> They tiptoed through the parlor
> on heavy, time-slowed feet.
> She watched him, from her front door,
> walk down the dawnlit street.
>
> Geneva was the wild one.
> Geneva was a tart.
> Geneva met a blue-eyed boy
> and gave away her heart.
>   (Ibid., 26–27)

"Of all the singers of Western lyric," Susan Stewart comments, "the ballad singer is the one most radically haunted by others."[30] "The Ballad of Aunt Geneva" celebrates this formal tradition that "Summer Storm" resists. A series of voices, not a private regret, haunts Nelson's ballad. It starts with the speaker rather impersonally introducing Geneva, classifying her according to type: "the wild one" and "a tart." The middle stanzas paraphrase the gossip that the community shares, as the speaker repeats what "[t]hey say." The poem's third part consists of a dramatic monologue, in which the poet ventriloquizes Geneva's magisterial insults. Geneva's brazenness reduces her lover to a secondary character, the auditor to her dramatic monologue:

> *I ain't got no time to waste*
> *on limp white mens like you.*
>
> *Oh yeah? Well, Mister White Man,*
> *it sure might be stone-white,*
> *but my thing's white as it is.*
> *And you know damn well I'm right.*

Following the dramatic monologue's conventions, a reader can infer the comparatively weak insults that the tellingly unnamed "old, white lover" unsuccessfully hurls at Geneva. In the space between these two stanzas, he defends what he might call his "manhood." Unfazed, Geneva inverts his claim of racial and gender superiority, turning "white" and "man" into slurs. "*Mister White Man*," she calls him. While the previous line's stress on "mens" suggests that the "limp" lover hardly qualifies as a man, the mock deference of "Mister," like the stress on "white," revises whiteness into a mark of racial inferiority. Finally, Geneva triumphantly outdoes her lover's crudeness, offering an even more outrageous genital comparison. Defeated, the lover can only mutely accept her insults: "*And you know damn well I'm right.*"

Appropriately, the different sections feature different rhythms. To revise Hughes's statement, some sections ask to be read aloud, others crooned, shouted, recited, and sung. Geneva's monologue employs suitably forceful rhythms, as many of the unstressed syllables receive strong secondary stresses. To detail how her "voice rang out," the section reproduces speech as reported in song; the insults snap at the rhymes and line breaks. For instance, the rhyme and line break in "on limp white mens like you" emphasize the contemptuous stress that Geneva places on "you." In contrast the last two stanzas reproduce much more tender rhythms. The cadences soften; the passage, like the characters it describes, moves with a new gentleness, "on heavy, time-slowed feet." The final stanza's artfulness repeats the words with a new inflection and resonance:

> Geneva was the wild one.
> Geneva was a tart.
> Geneva met a blue-eyed boy
> and gave away her heart.

Naming Geneva three times in four lines, the opening stanza summons her, first as the object of gossip, then as a voice to ventriloquize. The second stanza continues this pattern, naming Geneva twice in its first two lines. The same lines conclude the poem more ruminatively. As the poem's final, lingering rhyme, "tart" / "heart" suggests the pain Geneva privately bears, the part of her that the poet cannot recover and that the others cannot know.

Raunchy and profane, "The Ballad of Aunt Geneva" hardly seems to proffer the "righteous, praise Jesus song" that the homeplace demands, especially when compared with the poem that follows it. Describing the author's pilgrimage to her ancestral and spiritual "source of memory," the house where her great-grandparents lived, the book's opening poem explains the need it fulfills:

> [T]the homeplace moves me not to silence
> but to righteous, praise Jesus song:

Oh, catfish and turnip greens,
hot-water cornbread and grits.
Oh, musty, much-underlined Bibles;
generations lost to be found,
to be found.

(Waniek, *Homeplace*, 5)

The poem after "The Ballad of Aunt Geneva," "Aunt Annie's Prayer,"
imitates a call-and-response church hymn, ending simply

Praise God.
Thank You, Jesus.
Amen.
Amen.

(Ibid., 30)

Eminently respectable and devout, "Aunt Annie's Prayer," expresses
the conventional morality that Geneva scorns. Yet the poems' pairing
underscores the idea that the opening poem's colon punctuates: that
"righteous, praise Jesus song" arises from life's common pleasures
as well as sacred texts, from "catfish and turnip greens, / hot-water
cornbread and grits" as well as "musty, much-underlined Bibles." To
document her family history and to pay homage to it, Nelson employs
sacred and profane forms in quick succession. As her ballad implies,
"righteous, praise Jesus song" requires less the declaration of Christian
piety than praiseful rhythms. Praise comes in many forms, some
more obvious, such as the speaker's exclamations, "Oh," when she
imagines festive meals, some seemingly profane. The eighty-year-old
Geneva brings "her old, white lover in / to make love, and to fight";
their raucous insults intensify their sexual courtship, adding a kind of
postcoital verbal foreplay. The ballad form helps Nelson to frame the
poem as a text for performance, to intensify and modulate its cadences.
When the reader performs the print-based words, he or she discovers
that the rhythms exclaim an unexpected joy, the insults jubilant as "the
tell-tale / singing of the [bed] springs" (ibid., 26). Indeed, the reader's
performance clarifies Geneva's, showing that her banter slyly expresses
the tenderness she feels for her "old, white lover," the man she loves
and protects but can see only in private.

"The Ballad of Aunt Geneva" and "Summer Storm" illustrate two approaches to the ballad. Nelson's poem uses the form as a communal resource, a technique to make a private life public. It does so by employing verse rhythms that approach the cadences of song. Like the hymn Aunt Annie sings in church, "The Ballad of Aunt Geneva" presents words for performance. In contrast, "Summer Storm" uses the form to isolate a private moment, to add intimacy to an already-intimate address. To reverse Nelson's formulation, its whispery lyricism "move[s]" the reader closer to "silence" than to "song."

Anthologized in *Rebel Angels*, "Summer Storm" and "The Ballad of Aunt Geneva" represent a movement that Charles Bernstein has repeatedly criticized for aesthetic and political conservatism. A coeditor of L=A=N=G=U=A=G=E, Bernstein instead favors what he calls poetic "experiments" such as homophonic translations (translating a poem's sounds, not sense, into English) and "writing through" poems, which rewrite source texts.[31] When Bernstein uses metrical verse forms familiar to the English literary history, he generally parodies them. His most interesting poems, though, draw an oddly moving resonance from the forms they mock.

The penultimate poem in Bernstein's selected poems, "Rivulets of the Dead Jew" deftly employs doggerel technique:

Fill my plate with *boudin noir*
Boudin noir, boudin noir
Fill my plate with a hi-heh-ho
& rumble I will go

Don't dance with me
'til I cut my tie
Cut my tie, cut my tie
Don't fancy me 'til
The rivers run dry
& a heh & a hi & a ho

I've got a date with a
Bumble bee, bumble bee
I've got a date with a
wee bonnie wee
& ahurtling we will go.[32]

Bernstein has described his poetic method as "acting out, in dialectical play, the insincerity of form." Most contemporary poetry seeks to establish a credible speaking subject and illuminate his or her psychology. It prizes a consistency of tone and affect: what Bernstein would call a "sincerity of form." In contrast his work "collapses into a more ambivolent, destabilizing field of pathos, the ludicrous, schtick, sarcasm."³³

This "schtick" destabilizes the ballad form from within. "Rivulets of the Dead Jew" employs a dizzying number of formal references and allusions. The idioms it employs, such as "wee bonnie wee" and "Don't fancy me," recall English and Scottish folk ballads. Its refrains of "& ahurtling we will go" and "& rumble I will go" closely resemble those of hunting songs such as Fielding's "Hunting Song" and the anonymous lyric, "The Three Huntsmen," which respectively declare, "*And a-hunting we will go*" and "And a-hunting they did go."³⁴ "Rivulets of the Dead Jew" also presents a familiar ballad scene. In "The Last Goodnight" a character about to die offers a final farewell. This convention formed "a hackneyed standby" (Bold, *Ballad*, 37) of the broadside ballads merchants sold at public executions.

These many borrowings produce a seemingly incongruous pastiche of ballad technique. The title starts this process. "Rivulets of the Dead Jew" introduces a stock sentimental image, tearful and elegiac. The poem quickly turns on its title, presenting its clichés as clichés. As the first stanza soon makes clear, the "dead Jew" is not mournful but jubilant, hungry for the afterlife and its pleasures. Similarly, the poem's many idioms deliberately contradict each other. In a conventional "Last Goodbye" ballad, the condemned man achieves the grandeur of a doomed outlaw: an unrepentant sinner or a tragic figure whose moral conversion comes too late. "Rivulets of the Dead Jew" presents this villain as the comedian Mel Brooks might play him, mawkish, mock-heroic, and looking forward to a good meal.

As a parody of ballad conventions, "Rivulets of the Dead Jew" playfully rebukes contemporary writers of metrical verse. In one of Bernstein's memorable witticisms, he proposed "The Nude Formalism" to act as a "counter to a 'New Formalism' that claims a continuity with conventional lyric prosody but disdains its sonic excesses."³⁵ As part of this project, Bernstein advocates an alternative formal tradition, naming Hopkins, Skelton, and Swinburne as its major figures because their work foregrounds what Bernstein calls "the concrete particulars of sound and form over and against the dematerializing idea of voice or purity of expression." Such poetry, Bernstein claims, serves as a model for his own work: "Surely I use more of the tones and those high, swooning sounds from this tradition than many of my contemporaries" (ibid., 10).

The opening stanza offers a good example:

> Fill my plate with *boudin noir*
> *Boudin noir, boudin noir*
> Fill my plate with a hi-heh-ho
> & rumble I will go.

This stanza sets British, American, and French idioms to a galloping meter. To borrow Bernstein's terms, "sound and form" organize the stanza more than "voice or purity of expression." The opening phrase, "Fill my plate with," clearly establishes two patterns: a strong meter and an identifiable syntax. The stanza consists of two unpunctuated sentences, each of which assert the same command, "Fill my plate with . . ." This syntax functions as a kind of prosody, a signal that the reader should anticipate that the rest of sentence will answer the question, "Fill my plate with what?"[36] The stanza exploits the leeway these patterns allow. First, it introduces a "real" food that approaches nonsense, "*boudin noir*," hardly the dish that a "dead Jew" would be expected to demand. Second, it names a sound for the next dish: "a hi-heh-ho." This incremental repetition makes the strange seem familiar. To do so, the poem shifts from language's referential functions to its musical qualities; "a hi-heh-ho" presents a sound to sing, not denotes a food to eat.

As a criticism of new formalism, "Rivulets of the Dead Jew" highlights how contemporary verse often limits itself to a soft-spoken lyricism. In particular, the poem rebukes the mode of poetry that Gioia's ballad represents. Yet "Rivulets of the Dead Jew" does not fully account for Marilyn Nelson's ballad. Bernstein posits that to achieve "the tones and those high, swooning sounds" a poet must chose "the concrete particulars of sound and form *over and against* the dematerializing idea of voice or purity of expression" (my italics). "The Ballad of Aunt Geneva" features a sequence of speakers; it achieves a "sonic excess" without eschewing the notion of individual voice. Instead, a fidelity to these voices allows the poem to achieve its great tonal and rhythmic variety.

While implicitly critiquing new formalism, "Rivulets of the Dead Jew" paradoxically attests to metrical verse's continued possibilities. It draws from the first form that many readers encounter, usually before they can read. As Muriel Rukeyser wrote of Mother Goose, "We come to language through her."[37] The nursery rhyme acts as a powerful source text because children learn it early in life; it exists as a formative presence in the mind of those who heard it again and again before they could understand the rhyme's words. As usually printed, "Mary's Lamb" follows the common measure:

> Mary had a little lamb,
> Its fleece was white as snow;
> And everywhere that Mary went
> The lamb was sure to go.[38]

"[A]s ballads get farther and farther away from the people or from singing," George Kittredge has noted, "they tend to lose their refrains; the recited ballad has no need of them."[39] Tellingly, Bernstein's poem imitates the form that "Mary's Lamb" takes when sung, not recited:

> Mary had a little lamb,
> Little lamb, little lamb,
> Mary had a little lamb,
> Its fleece was white as snow.
> And everywhere that Mary went
> Mary went, Mary went,
> And everywhere that Mary went
> The lamb was sure to go.

"Rivulets of the Dead Jew" echoes "Mary's Lamb" at the form's most conspicuous places: the opening and close of the first stanza. The first two lines

> Fill my plate with *boudin noir*
> *Boudin noir, boudin noir*

perfectly reproduce this meter, as does the stanza's last line, "& rumble I will go," whose rhyme also echoes the sung version of "Mary's Lamb." The opening stanza, then, starts and finishes with the form's distinctive techniques.

Echoing a specific nursery rhyme, "Rivulets of the Dead Jew" follows a precedent. Most famously, Elizabeth Bishop's "Visits to St. Elizabeths" and Donald Justice's "Counting the Mad" respectively draw from "The House that Jack Built" and "This Little Pig" to dramatize the experience of an insane asylum, what Bishop calls Bedlam's peculiar "time."[40] In the two earlier poems, the nursery rhyme form achieves two main effects. First, it comments on the poem's action, adding a sometimes-ironic counterpoint to the depicted action. Second, it adds an inescapable rhythm rich with associations. In order to experience the poem fully, a reader not only must recognize the source text but also feel a startling discrepancy. The rhythm that evokes an asylum's terrors must summon a gentle memory: a singing parent wiggling her child's toes. If the reader lacks this association, the nursery rhyme works as an intellectual reference, not a common experience.

Bernstein treats the nursery rhyme far less reverentially than Justice and Bishop do, jumbling it with a number of other sources. Yet the form helps "Rivulets of the Dead Jew" achieve an emotional resonance missing in some of Bernstein's other works. While echoing a nursery rhyme, "Rivulets of the Dead Jew" reverses the effect that Justice's and Bishop's poems achieve. Their poems echo nursery rhymes in order to express the depicted scene's strangeness, the difference between the patients' self-perceptions and the observer's knowledge of them. In Justice's poem, the final stanza catalogues what each patient "thought himself" to be: a "bird," "dog," and "man."[41] The nursery rhyme form insists on the patients' helpless, child-like state; it suggests the patients' estrangement from the lives that sane people enjoy. In "Rivulets of the Dead Jew," the speaker, "the dead Jew," readies himself for the afterlife. Like the madman's assertions, his words are otherworldly, some literally nonsense, "Fill my plate with a hi-heh-ho." The form of "Rivulets of the Dead Jew" evokes a point of contact, not misunderstanding. Death remains the greatest mystery because, by definition, the living cannot know it. The poem's verse form, though, evokes the familial and social relations that "dead Jew" once knew, the scenes where parents sang nursery rhymes to their children. The speaker lusts for the afterlife, his "date," but the poem's form recalls the life and the loved ones he leaves behind. It suggests that this poem should be read as an elegy to a father, complete with the ambivalence that a father's death might inspire.

"Rivulets of the Dead Jew" encourages contemporary poets to venture beyond a familiar range of sounds and of voices, to leave the dulled, conversational tones and explore the full range of possibilities that a form such as the ballad offers. Together with the sestinas, sonnets, ghazals, and couplets I have discussed, the poem demonstrates the opportunities that metrical forms offer. They function as a kind of shorthand, clarifying the present situation with echoes of the past. As in "Rivulets of the Dead Jew," verse form sets the poem in a recognizable human context. It reveals the affinities that contemporaries share, even though they "belong" to different poetic camps. Finally, as always "ahurtling" toward an uncertain future, the new poem disorients the form, claiming a new context and a different imperative.

When I taught "Rivulets of the Dead Jew" in an introduction to poetry class, I asked the students to perform the poem in whatever manner they thought best. Two sang it plaintively as if it were a sentimental Irish elegy. Another rapped the words, using staccato rhythms and sweeping her hand as if she were a deejay scratching a record. Most surprisingly, a student stood atop her desk, sang the poem and exuberantly danced. Her performance framed the poem as a high-spirited farewell to life and a jubilant welcome to death's sublime "date."

In the subsequent discussion, the students explained the reasons, intuitions, and interpretations that inspired them to perform the poem as they did. As in our other meetings, they marshaled textual evidence to defend their analysis. The shy tentativeness that characterized previous discussions, though, remained strikingly absent. The performances emboldened the students by allowing them to inhabit the poem. Prosody is often thought of as a contract between poem and reader, a set of obligations each must follow. Like the ballad that inspired it, the class discussion suggested another prospect: that prosody provides reader and writer alike with the means to explore, not resolve, the language's and the culture's ever shifting possibilities, a circumstance that rewards curiosity and punishes dogmatism.

CONCLUSION

PROSODY AFTER THE POETRY WARS

Phil I'm so happy to be a contemporary: happy to share
the language. Tho they climb only the stairway of lost
breath, they lion come It is astonishing how they lion
come—Mary and I reading the books all afternoon—
—George Oppen, letter to Philip Levine, 1974

SHREWD POETS ARE OPPORTUNISTS, DRAWING FROM DIVERSE INFLUENCES.
Their wanderlust frustrates those who seek to map uncomplicated lines
of affiliation. In my epigraph, George Oppen hails a rather surprising
"contemporary," a poet soon fated to serve as one of the avant-garde's
customary targets of abuse. Oppen's brief prose poem celebrates the
"books" that he and his wife Mary have enjoyed "all afternoon," adding
his distinctive spacing to Philip Levine's "astonishing" words.[1] Robert
Duncan's manuscripts illustrate a more extensive collaboration. They
show how Thom Gunn's book, *Moly*, provoked Duncan to draft a series
of poems in the margins alongside Gunn's syllabic verse. A meditation
on *Moly*, Duncan's sequence borrows certain phrases, rhythms, and
a mythological framework, using the space that Gunn's poetry leaves.
"Irregular meters beat between your heart and mine," Duncan writes,
addressing Gunn.[2] Duncan could not have made the connection
more visible, naming his sequence "Poems from the Margins of Thom
Gunn's *Moly*."[3]

The 1994 anthology *From the Other Side of the Century: A New
American Poetry 1960–1990* contains more than one thousand pages
of poetry, including Duncan's "Preface to the Suite," but not Gunn's
poem that inspired it, twelve pages of Oppen's work, but none written
by the poet with whom he was "happy to share the language." Such

omissions split a diverse literary culture into two halves, each of which pretends that the other exists only as its foil. Too many valedictions to "the poetry wars" play slight changes on this pattern, confirming the metaphor's remarkable tenacity, its ability to guide even the discussions that putatively reject it. A collection of essays considers the state of American poetry "After New Formalism"; a symposium contemplates the same situation "After Language."[4] Neither explores the possibilities that exist "after"—and between—*both* movements.

Prosody after "the poetry wars" demands a less antagonistic, more nuanced model of creativity, one capable of acknowledging how writers echo even the ideas they dispute. Unless we wish to repeat what the poet Greg Williamson calls "a hundred years of bickering" about poetic form,[5] we need a critical vocabulary that clarifies the era's most interesting poetry, instead of ignoring it. I propose we discuss "contemporaries" who "share the language," not partisans who wage "wars."

Consider, for instance, H. L. Hix's remarkable sequence, "Orders of Magnitude." Collected in *Rational Numbers* (2000), it consists of one hundred ten-line sections, with ten syllables per line. Hix's term for the sections, "decimals," emphasizes that each one-hundred-syllable part offers a numerical microcosm of the whole. A section just past the middle suggests some of the effects that the poem's allusive style and numerical form achieve:

> Let me start over. Not so I can speak
> clearly, but so I can mimic the gods.
> When they command the wind the wind obeys
> its own will. I understand the devil's
> one melodious truth but not the gods'
> polyphonic paradox. Not so I
> can say something else, but so I can mean
> more by the same thing, more than I meant then,
> more than I can know I mean now. More than
> the gods, who understand all but themselves.[6]

Like the sequence's shifting, provisional, and fractured points of view, its allusions eerily undercut the notion of individual voice. Informed by the attribution page, the reader knows that each section "incorporates a (sometimes manipulated) fragment of text from another source" (ibid., xi). Yet even the most omnivorous reader lacks sufficient information to identify the source text, especially since "Orders of Magnitude" borrows obscure fragments whose meaning it dramatically revises. This decimal draws from *"Honey in the Rock,"* a collection of African American religious folk songs that Ruby Pickens Tartt compiled in Sumter County, Alabama, from the early 1930s to the early 1950s. "Ananias, Ananias" starts with the line that Hix revises, as Saul addresses Ananias, who has miraculously restored his sight:

> He spoke ter de win,' en de win' obey,
> Tell me whut kind uv er man Jesus is;
> Ananias, Ananias, tell me whut kind er man Jesus is.[7]

Awestruck, Saul praises Jesus' powers. As the musicologists Olivia and Jack Solomon note, Saul's questions "carry not a tinge of doubt—they are, rather, affirmations of faith" (ibid., 126).

Revising the song's opening line, Hix reverses its meaning, "When they command the wind the wind obeys / its own will." Instead of celebrating a god's accomplishments, he considers the powerlessness that the plural "gods" suffer. With a careful feint, the enjambment invokes the idea that it renounces. After the speaker expresses a desire to assume god-like control, the line break reveals that the power to command others is exactly what the speaker does not want and what the gods lack. "When they command the wind the wind obeys" its own will, not the gods' decree. The other sections borrow fragments from either obscure sources or obscure passages of more famous sources. This decimal pursues the first strategy. Inspired by a relatively unknown collection of religious folk lyrics, not, say, a biblical verse, it avoids the standards that more readers might recognize.[8] Because the decimal carefully hides its source, it would have been nearly impossible for me to discover which line originates from another text, let alone the name of that source, without the poet's response to my query.

In this respect, my analysis retreats from the most powerful reading experience that "Orders of Magnitude" inspires. By manipulating obscure fragments, "Orders of Magnitude" does not present puzzles that the reader should "solve" by doggedly hunting down the source texts nor tests of cultural literacy that divide the learned from the ignorant. The reader instead possesses the broader but no less pointed knowledge that another text generated each section, even those that dramatize moments of seemingly personal revelation. Hix's phrase, "polyphonic paradox," nicely captures the dynamic that results. The sources exist as an eerie, shifting fact, a presence that haunts the reader's experience because he cannot evaluate either their relevance or the severity of Hix's manipulations. The reader experiences this multivoiced text as "polyphonic," a multitude encountered as a single, complete whole.

Echoing this paradox, "Orders of Magnitude" uses an extremely logical structure to explore the limits of rationality. The decimals in *Rational Numbers* follow an elegantly symmetrical mathematical progression: one hundred sections of ten ten-syllable lines. This orderly progression frames horrible scenes of sadistic violence, human and divine. It alludes to a god-like symmetry, but one that has lost all of its authority except to inflict pain. As one decimal notes, there has never been a god and he will "crush you / as he crushed your father and your father's / father" (Hix, *Rational Numbers*, 12). Poetic form provides the means to transform this grim truth. As Hix elsewhere notes, "Great poems speak with greater wisdom than the poets who wrote them possessed. The catalysis for such alchemy comes from form."[9] In the poem's terms, the form imposes "a will" that resists the poet's. For this paradoxical reason, the poet seeks to "mimic the gods," asserting his "command" so it will be disobeyed. The challenge is to develop a form strong enough to defy his intent, so he might express "more than I can know I mean."

A ten-syllable line cannot help but allude to iambic pentameter, the language's most famous meter and the one most often linked to speech. "Orders of Magnitude" converts this celebrated line into a mathematical formula, an abstraction. This form might be called claustrophobic, as it punishes any attempts at transcendence, enforcing what another section calls a "painful rigidity" (Hix, *Rational Numbers*, 36).

"I understand," the speaker declares, introducing the decimal's flashiest formal gesture

> the devil's
> one melodious truth but not the gods'
> polyphonic paradox. Not so I
> can say something else, but so I can mean
> more by the same thing, more than I meant then,
> more than I can know I mean now. More than . . .

The phrase "polyphonic paradox" dominates the passage's third line, claiming seven of its ten syllables. Consisting of four consecutive trochees (the last tailless), the phrase asserts a bold rhythm, the sound of the very "paradox" the speaker wishes to know. After the medial caesura, only three syllables remain. One option would be to use a single, three-syllable word, say, "Transcendent," adding another flourish to finish the line and start the next sentence. The poem instead solves the technical challenge austerely, with a gesture the subsequent lines repeat. It uses three one-syllable words, an increasingly modest, pinched, and repetitive vocabulary, culminating in two lines comprised entirely of one-syllable words. It retreats, as if chastised by the form.

This dynamic makes the experience of reading "Orders of Magnitude" extremely disturbing. "I have not said what I wanted to say," the sequence ends (ibid., 36). This lament can be read as a perverse boast, an assertion that the speaker has fulfilled his determination to "mean" "more than I can know I mean." "Orders of Magnitude" relentlessly fractures the poetic self so it might gain wisdom. In an obsessive quest to break its own will, the poem follows a nearly inhuman pattern, a numerical progression that defies the critical assumption that discernible speech patterns define meter. This technique suggests obvious affinities with the concerns of contemporary avant-garde verse; the poem's key phrase, "polyphonic paradox," pithily characterizes a familiar mode of much contemporary poetry, a disjunctive, dissonant poetics that resists neat closure. "Orders of Magnitude," though, lacks a sense of its own groundbreaking heroism; unlike the polemics for the new formalism and L=A=N=G=U=A=G=E Writing, it never claims to advance some liberatory project. "Orders of Magnitude" instead dramatizes how quickly writing procedures grow into compulsions, systems that perpetuate their obsessions rather than generate serviceable models for cultural transformation. "Thought is a form of grief," Hix declares in his study of postmodern theory, *Spirits Hovering over the Ashes: Legacies of Postmodern Theory* (1995).[10] After noting that earlier philosophers had transformed similar laments into ideals of virtue, Hix concludes, "It remains to be seen whether any postmodern theorist will have the force of character to forge such a powerful ideal for our new situation and our new selves" (ibid., 25). "Orders of Magnitude" hovers over postmodernity's ashes, over the art and philosophy that powerfully expressed but failed to solve the problems that the era presented.

Published two years after Hix's *Rational Numbers*, Jennifer Moxley's *The Sense Record and Other Poems* (2002) shares an interest in using techniques that literary criticism assigns to separate poetic camps. A pair of meditations upon formal technique bookend the collection. "My thoughts are too awkward, too erratic to rest / at ease in the beautiful iamb," the first poem declares, explaining:

> The poem therefore must be
> a fit
>   condolence, a momentary
> and ordered form of the emphatic
>   question, around which continues to gather,
> *despite habitual despair,*
>   the moving
> and needful Company of
>   thought, attentive
> to existence, quiet and ever
>   perpetual.[11]

As the coeditor of "The Impercipient Lecture Series," Moxley helped publish Bob Perelman's poem "Confession," a parody of his poetic development.[12] The poem describes aliens—"egg-headed, tentacled, slimier-than-thou aestheticians"—who convert confessional poets into avant-garde writers; they "abduct naive poets, and / inculcate them with otherworldly forms." In an interview, Perelman explained how the poem expresses his ambivalence about the notion of the avant-garde. Dual purposes inspired the poem, which sought to "confer a transcendental gloss on the avant-garde by saying that it's otherwordly, heavenly, in this case, alien" and to "conflate it [the avant-garde] with fashion design of the most nugatory order." As such, the poem offers an insider's critique of the avant-garde, as Perelman witnessed how L=A=N=G=U=A=G=E Writing inspired outrage then cooptation. The form he employs seeks to express the movement's initial contrariness, its opposition stance, even to itself. To explore this double-mindedness, Perelman wrote couplets whose lines contain six words, a technique he calls "anti-vatic, anti-shamanistic, anti-Projective verse, anti-sonic authenticity, anti-iambic-pentameter-RSC-British-heritage, etc."[13]

Perelman's "otherworldly form" establishes a long string of antagonisms. As if it could go on forever, his list of foes ends with "etc."

Moxley's "otherworldly metrics" claim a series of affinities. Earlier in the poem, she borrows an image from "Of Being Numerous"; the poem's spacing also pays homage to Oppen, using the page's blank spaces to control intonation, stress, and cadence. Oppen criticized poets who employed "the line-ending simply as the ending of the line." "The meaning of a poem," Oppen asserted, "is in the cadences and the shape of the lines and the pulse of the thought which is given by those lines."[14]

Moxley's lines heed Oppen's advice. Consider what happens to the "pulse" of their "thought" when they are rearranged:

> The poem therefore must be a fit condolence,
> a momentary and ordered form of the
> emphatic question, around which continues to gather,
> *despite habitual despair*, the moving
> and needful Company of thought, attentive
> to existence, quiet and ever perpetual.

The opening line undergoes the most dramatic change. "The poem therefore must be a fit condolence" offers a confident assertion. Broken into three lines, it presents the rhythm of self-questioning, a halting, meditative working-out of what "[t]he poem" "must be." The poem's confident rhetoric includes the syllogistic "therefore," a suggestion that the speaker follows an already mapped argument. Moxley's arrangement transfers words in and out of grammatical positions and meanings. "The poem therefore must be / a fit"—a petulant expression of outrage. The next line changes the noun into an adjective that means nearly the opposite; "a fit / condolence" expresses a respectful sensitivity, not a self-indulgent tantrum. As in Moxley's arrangement, the majority of the rearranged lines are enjambed, but to very different effect. The enjambment in my version—"*despite habitual despair, the moving*"—speeds the reader to the next line. Moxley's version works toward a subtler end. Enjambed but isolated, "the moving" propels the reader's attention into the blank space that surrounds it. It demands a certain attentiveness, a focus on the parts of speech and the argumentative elements that a more uniform arrangement might hide. Instead of a smooth argument, it presents a series of "momentary / and ordered" explorations.

This rearrangement also foregrounds the lines' loose blank verse base. More than a half-century after Pound's retrospective blast, Moxley does not seek "to break the pentameter"; she uses it as an underlying order, a half-hidden means to shape the "momentary."[15] The poet putatively renounces the "iamb," only to praise it. Drawn to the meter again and again, the poem finds it alluringly attractive, a contrast to its own "awkward thoughts." Like any object of desire, the "beautiful iamb" inspires ambivalence: feelings of inadequacy and reverence, denunciation and praise.

The book's final poem, "The Just Real," clarifies these formal concerns, declaring:

> I did not ask for rhyme, but there it came,
> I did not wish to speak of grief but grief
> refused my silence, in art I sought strife,
> in love, passion, but found instead a strange
> event of artifice and comfort. I'm . . .
>   (Moxley, *Sense Record*, 77)

In an era that regularly praises art as "weird" and "disturbing," the idea that technique also brings "comfort" seems almost shocking. Building to this odd revelation, the passage eroticizes artistic technique, comparing it to "love" because neither obeys rational choice. As a pun relates, "rhyme," though unasked, "came." Like Hix, Moxley argues that artistic technique "refuses" the poet's will. Unlike the paranoid "Orders of Magnitude," "The Just Real" shows how "artifice" and "comfort" coincide, and how one might inspire the other.

Demonstrating this idea, the passage's first two lines feature a rather strict, insistent meter. This blank verse uses only monosyllabic words; grammatically dominant parts of speech such as nouns and verbs command the stressed positions, while prepositions fill several unstressed positions. The passage's next line also contains ten syllables, but the meter roughens midway through it. After the opening two iambs, the line turns metrically irregular. "[R]efused my silence, in art I sought strife" might be scanned as ending either with an ionic foot then a spondee or an anapest then a bacchic, which would give the line just four feet.[16] Following this unusual construction, the next line inverts the second foot. In the space of seven syllables, the poem places substitutions in the two unlikeliest positions: the final and the second. But just as the poem seems to reproduce a kind of formal "strife," a metrical regularity returns. The second half of the passage's fourth line uses the opening line's technique, employing a simple diction and a clear alignment of metrical position and grammatical importance. Reestablishing the iambic pentameter base, these techniques make the half-line, "but found instead a strange," nearly as metrically insistent as the passage's opening. The passage closes with a line whose meter remains neither insistently regular nor harshly irregular. The line, "event of artifice and comfort. I'm," strictly adheres to the iambic pentameter pattern, but features a greater syntactic and rhythmic flexibility. The final caesura divides the last foot, counterpointing meter and rhythm. The line also employs a wider range of relative stress. Because of its metrical position, the final syllable in "artifice" receives a stress, but hardly the strong attention that each alternative syllable in the first two lines demands.

These metrical tricks present several kinds of blank verse. The opening two lines seem as grimly controlled as the poet who tries to command herself to renounce "rhyme" and expressions of "grief." The middle lines present a similarly willful determination, this time to seek "strife" and "passion." If the opening lines seem almost monotonously regular, the middle lines seem self-consciously rough. The last line, though, presents a moment of formal revelation, an "event," in which "artifice" and "control" balance each other.

Praising Moxley's work, Ron Silliman questions why she is often classified as a member of "the newer generation of post-avant writing," not a "master" of "traditional stylistics." Silliman proposes a number of explanations, including Moxley's friendships with other younger "post-avant" writers, before concluding that "the reason" is "her work *déjà toujours* presumes the context of post-avant writing."[17] In a limited sense, Silliman is correct: Moxley self-consciously writes after not only Modernism but also L=A=N=G=U=A=G=E Writing and new formalism.[18] Yet the same might also be said of Hix. When discussed at all, he finds himself called a practitioner of "traditional stylistics," not a member of "the newer generation of post-avant writing." If Hix had received a Ph.D. from SUNY Buffalo, not the University of Texas, his work would enjoy a very different readership.

Clumsy and indiscriminate, the terms "traditional stylistics" and "post-avant writing" reflect the state of thinking on the subject. A new generation *has* emerged; one need only to read Hix's work beside Gioia's, and Moxley's beside Perelman's, to see the difference. Gioia favorably reviewed Hix's first book, which earned little other attention, and picked his second for publication, and Moxley has named Perelman as a crucial influence. The younger poets tend to place different traditions in dialogue, not pit them in competition. Instead of manufacturing another "poetry war," they present themselves as a generation, as in Peter Gizzi's poetic parable, which describes children playing in a street: "their game will become an entire century."[19]

In order to do so, this poetry rereads its predecessors.' When Moxley borrows an image from "Of Being Numerous," she simply assumes that the reader shares her reverence for Oppen's work. She does not seek to recuperate the poet; she takes Oppen's canonical status for granted.

This strategy would make little sense until recently. For too long criticism remained content to call Oppen an objectivist, without acknowledging how little that term explained his work. Many contemporary poets find themselves in a similar bind, assigned to movements that erase their works' most vital, idiosyncratic explorations. If, as Moxley predicts, "[T]o future generations of readers, invisible distinctions will become glaringly obvious,"[20] criticism's task is to expedite this process, to illuminate unseen sympathies as well as distinctions. Attention to the particular forms that poets favor and those they neglect offers one means to this end; it makes certain family resemblances "glaringly obvious" and other classifications seem rather contrived. Careful readers will note that the names of many usual suspects do not appear in this study while others have been relegated to endnotes or asides. Poets commonly treated as tokens or minor figures receive extensive attention. While space restrictions necessitate many omissions, my intent is to shift focus from writers of the most provocative polemics to poets who compose the most interesting verse. A few authors possess the rare ability to do both, but even their partisan blasts unwittingly offer another reason not to pay attention to the complications that make poetic form fascinating, another rationalization to read and teach even less poetry. Why bother with Thom Gunn's elegy to a friend dying of AIDS-related complications or Derek Walcott's calypso-inflected couplets when one of the most sensitive readers of contemporary poetry confirms that "the very appearance of heroic couplets" "is a signifier of 'light verse,' something fun and parodic, not meant to be taken too seriously"?[21] Earlier I quoted Hix's observation that poetic form allows "[g]reat poems to speak with greater wisdom than the poets who wrote them possessed" (Hix, *Easy as Lying*, 50). This is more than an *ars poetica*; it is a challenge to develop the strategies, patience, and openness necessary to access this wisdom.

NOTES

Introduction

1. Antony Easthope, *Poetry as Discourse* (London: Methuen and Company, 1983), 76.

2. Ira Sadoff, "Neo-Formalism: A Dangerous Nostalgia," *American Poetry Review* 19, no. 1 (January–February 1990): 7–13; Diane Wakoski, "The New Conservatism in American Poetry," *American Book Review* 8, no. 4 (May–June 1986): 3.

Anthologies provide the most conspicuous evidence of an increased interest in metrical verse. See Philip Dacey and David Jauss, *Strong Measures: Contemporary American Poetry in Traditional Forms* (New York: Harper and Row, 1986); Robert Richman, ed., *The Direction of Poetry: An Anthology of Rhymed and Metered Verse Written in the English Language since 1975* (Boston: Houghton Mifflin, 1988); Annie Finch, ed., *A Formal Feeling Comes: Poems in Form by Contemporary Women* (Brownsville, Ore.: Story Line Press, 1994); and Mark Jarman and David Mason, eds., *Rebel Angels: 25 Poets of the New Formalism* (Brownsville, Ore.: Story Line Press, 1996).

3. Jerome Rothenberg and Pierre Joris, eds., *Poems for the Millennium: The University of California Book of Modern and Postmodern Poetry* (Berkeley: University of California Press, 1998), 2:3.

4. On this point, see Robert Scholes, *The Fabulators* (Oxford: Oxford University Press, 1967); Ralph Cohen, "Do Postmodern Genres Exist?" in *Postmodern Genres*, ed. Marjorie Perloff (Norman: University of Oklahoma Press, 1989), 11–27; and Milan Kundera, *Testaments Betrayed: An Essay in Nine Parts*, trans. Linda Asher (New York: HarperCollins, 1996), 74–76.

5. *Going Forth by Day*, exhibition catalogue (Berlin: Deutsche Guggenheim, 2002), 94. Viola lists Botticelli's drawings of the Inferno and Purgatory, the Egyptian Book of the Dead, and Luca Signorelli's Orvieto Cathedral fresco cycle as other influences for *Going Forth by Day*.

6. James Gleick, *Faster: The Acceleration of Just About Everything* (New York: Pantheon Books, 1999), 79.

7. Primo Levi, "Rhyming on the Counterattack," in *The Mirror Maker: Stories and Essays*, trans. Raymond Rosenthal (New York: Schocken Books, 1989), 112, 113.

8. Jorge Luis Borges, *Borges on Writing*, ed. Norman Thomas di Giovanni, Daniel Halpern, and Frank MacShane (Hopewell, N.J.: Ecco Press, 1994), 71, 74–75.

9. Jennifer Trainer, ed., *MASS MoCA: From Mill to Museum* (North Adams, Mass.: MASS MoCA Publications, 2000), 16.

10. Adrienne Rich, "Claiming and Education," in *On Lies, Secrets, and Silence: Selected Prose, 1966–1978* (New York: W. W. Norton, 1979), 231–35.

11. T. S. Eliot, *Selected Prose of T. S. Eliot*, ed. Frank Kermode (New York: Harcourt Brace Jovanovich, 1975), 35–36.

12. Dacey and Jauss, *Strong Measures*, 13.

13. In a 1970 interview, Donald Justice insisted he would not be interested in writing sonnets. When Justice edited the interview in 1983, his footnote wryly confirmed that he had "conquered" this "prejudice." See Donald Justice, *Platonic Scripts* (Ann Arbor: University of Michigan Press, 1984), 17.

14. Jorie Graham, "That Glorious Thing." Interview with Mark Wunderlich. *American Poet* (fall 1996); The Academy of American Poets. www.poets.org/poems/prose. cfm?45442B7C000C070D0876 (accessed December 15, 1999).

15. Martin Corless-Smith, untitled interview with Rick Snyder. *Read Me* 4 (spring–summer 2001). www.home.jps.net/~nada/corless.htm. See also Martin Corless-Smith, *Complete Travels* (Sheffield: White House Books, 2000), 71–96.

16. Timothy Steele, *All the Fun's in How You Say a Thing: An Explanation of Meter and Versification* (Athens: Ohio University Press, 1999); Alfred Corn, *The Poem's Heartbeat: A Manual of Prosody* (Brownsville, Ore.: Story Line Press, 1997); Mark Strand and Eavan Boland, eds., *The Making of a Poem: A Norton Anthology of Poetic Forms* (New York: W. W. Norton, 2000); Charles Bernstein, *The Politics of Poetic Form: Poetry and Public Policy* (New York: Roof Books, 1990); Annie Finch, ed., *After New Formalism: Poets on Form, Narrative, and Tradition* (Ashland, Ore.: Story Line Press, 1999); R. S. Gwynn, ed., *New Expansive Poetry: Theory, Criticism, History* (Ashland, Ore.: Story Line Press, 1999); Annie Finch and Kathrine Varnes, eds., *An Exaltation of Forms: Contemporary Poets Celebrate the Diversity of Their Art* (Ann Arbor: University of Michigan Press, 2002); David Baker, ed., *Meter in English: A Critical Engagement* (Fayetteville: University of Arkansas Press, 1996); and Dana Gioia, David Mason, and Meg Shoerke, eds., *Twentieth-Century American Poetics: Poets on the Art of Poetry* (New York: McGraw-Hill, 2004).

17. Cary Nelson, *Our Last First Poets: Vision and History in Contemporary American Poetry* (Urbana: University of Illinois Press, 1981), ix; Charles Bernstein, *A Poetics* (Cambridge: Harvard University Press, 1992); Bernstein, *Content's Dream: Essays, 1975–1984* (Los Angeles: Sun and Moon Press, 1986); Bernstein, *My Way: Speeches and Poems* (Chicago: University of Chicago Press, 1999); Marjorie Perloff, *The Poetics of Indeterminacy: Rimbaud to Cage* (Princeton, N.J.: Princeton University Press, 1981). See also Marjorie Perloff, "The Return of the (Numerical) Repressed," in *Radical Artifice: Writing Poetry in the Age of Media* (Chicago: University of Chicago Press, 1991), 134–70, especially 134–36; and Perloff, "'A Step Away from Them': Poetry 1956," in *Poetry On*

& Off the Page: Essays for Emergent Occasions (Evanston, Ill.: Northwestern University Press, 1998), 83–115.

Two studies of contemporary poetic form have been especially helpful to me. Mutlu Konuk Blasing's *Politics and Form in Postmodern Poetry: O'Hara, Bishop, Ashbery, and Merrill* (Cambridge: Cambridge University Press, 1995) anticipates my distaste for the easy elision of metrical verse with conservative politics and "experimental" forms with political opposition. Yet Blasing's reading of individual poets differs from my readings of poetic forms by taking as a "[g]iven the political neutrality of technical options" (17) while my study explores the changing political and aesthetic implications of certain poetic forms. As my chapter of the heroic couplet indicates, James Longenbach's interrogation of "the 'breakthrough' narrative" in *Modern Poetry after Modernism* (New York: Oxford University Press, 1997) echoes some of my own suspicions about the critical reception of metrical and free verse, though my subject is not "modern poetry after Modernism" but contemporary poetry's metrical forms.

18. Billy Collins, "American Sonnet," in *Sailing Alone around the Room: New and Selected Poems* (New York: Random House, 2001), 23.

19. Gerald Stern, *American Sonnets* (New York: W. W. Norton, 2002).

20. Claude McKay, *A Long Way from Home* (New York: Harcourt, Brace and World, 1970), 21, 31–32.

21. Senate, *Investigation Activities of the Department of Justice*, 66th Cong., 1st sess., S. Doc. 153, 167. Lodge is quoted in Lloyd W. Brown, *West Indian Poetry* (Boston: Twayne Publishers, 1978), 39. The black press quickly learned of the Department of Justice's monitoring. See "We 'Rile' the Crackerized Department of Justice," *Crusader* 2, no. 9 (May 1920): 5–6.

22. Melvin B. Tolson, "Claude McKay's Art," *Poetry* 83, no. 5 (February 1954): 287; McKay's comments on "If We Must Die," *Anthology of Negro Poetry*, Folkway Records Album No. FL 9791. The often-repeated story of Churchill reading the poem has two main versions. The first suggests that, as Arna Bontemps writes, Churchill "quoted it ['If We Must Die'] as the conclusion to his address before the joint houses of Congress prior to the entrance of the United States into World War II." This story is told in Arna Bontemps, ed., introduction to *American Negro Poetry* (New York: Hill and Wang, 1963), xvi; and Tyrone Tillery, *Claude McKay: A Black Poet's Struggle for Identity* (Amherst: University of Massachusetts Press, 1992), 35. Churchill's December 26, 1941, speech, though, makes no such mention of McKay's poem. The second and more common version is harder either to verify or to disprove. It suggests that Churchill read the poem sometime during World War II at the House of Commons. A specific date is never mentioned. This version is especially popular with black poets. See Tolson (supra, this note); Gwendolyn Brooks, letter to the editor, *Time* 98, no. 16 (October 18, 1971): 6; Michael S. Harper and Anthony Walton, eds., *The Vintage Book of African American Poetry* (New York: Vintage Books, 2000), 99; and Robert Hayden, ed., *Kaleidoscope: Poems by American Negro Poets* (New York: Harcourt, Brace and World, 1967), 45. Wayne Cooper claims Churchill never read the poem to the House of Commons; David Perkins writes that the poem may have "stirred the Edwardian heart of Winston Churchill, who is said to have read it in the House of Commons"; and Jean Wagner writes "it seems true" "but we have no confirmation of this." See Wayne F. Cooper, review of *Claude McKay*:

A Black Poet's Struggle for Identity, by Tyrone Tillery, *Journal of American History* 79, no. 4 (1993): 1656–1757; David Perkins, *A History of Modern Poetry,* vol. 1, *From the 1890s to the High Modernist Mode* (Cambridge: Harvard University Press, 1976), 404; Jean Wagner, *Black Poets of the United States: From Paul Lawrence Dunbar to Langston Hughes,* trans. Kenneth Douglas (Urbana: University of Illinois Press, 1973), 230, n. 95. None of these accounts cite a specific date for Churchill's recitation of the poem. I can find no mention of McKay's poem in Robert Rhodes James, ed., *Winston S. Churchill: His Complete Speeches, 1897–1963* (New York: Chelsea House Publishers, 1974), or in Churchill scholarship. Regardless of whether or not Churchill actually read the poem to the House of Commons or quoted it in some other occasion, the currency that this story has achieved makes it an important part of the poem's reception.

23. "War in Attica: Was There No Other Way?" *Time* 98, no. 13 (September 27, 1971): 20.

24. Gwendolyn Brooks, letter to the editor, *Time* 98, no. 16 (October 18, 1971): 6.

25. Nathan Irvin Huggins notes that when "If We Must Die" was published "in the *Messenger* in 1919 and in *Harlem Shadows* in 1922 no one could doubt that the author was a black man and the 'we' of the poem black people too." See Nathan Irvin Huggins, *Harlem Renaissance* (New York: Oxford University Press, 1971), 72.

26. Claude McKay, "Author's Word" in *Harlem Shadows: The Poems of Claude McKay* (New York: Harcourt, Brace and Company, 1922), xx.

27. Houston A. Baker Jr., *Modernism and the Harlem Renaissance* (Chicago: University of Chicago Press, 1987), 87.

28. Claude McKay, "Boyhood in Jamaica," *Phylon* 13 (spring 1953): 142.

29. Melvin B. Tolson, "Claude McKay's Art," 289.

30. Lloyd Schwartz and Sybil P. Estess, eds., *Elizabeth Bishop and Her Art* (Ann Arbor: University of Michigan Press, 1983), 293.

31. John Ashbery, *Selected Poems* (New York: Penguin Books, 1985), 208–9; Lyn Hejinian, *My Life,* rev. ed. (Los Angeles: Sun and Moon Press, 1991), 48.

Chapter 1

1. See Elizabeth Bishop, "A Miracle for Breakfast," *Poetry: A Magazine of Verse* 50, no. 4 (July 1937): 182–84; I use the version from Bishop's *The Complete Poems 1927–1979* (New York: Farrar, Straus and Giroux, 1992), 18–19, which makes only very minor changes.

2. Lloyd Schwartz and Sybil P. Estess, eds., *Elizabeth Bishop and Her Art* (Ann Arbor: University of Michigan Press, 1983), 297.

3. W. H. Auden, *Collected Poems,* ed. Edward Mendelson (London: Faber and Faber, 1991), 119; Louis Zukofsky, *All the Collected Short Poems, 1923–1964* (New York: W. W. Norton, 1971), 74.

4. Humphrey Carpenter, *A Serious Character: The Life of Ezra Pound* (Boston: Houghton Mifflin Company, 1988), 116, 109; and Ezra Pound, *The Selected Poems of Ezra Pound* (New York: New Directions Books, 1957), 7. "Technically it is one of my best," Pound claimed of "Sestina: Altaforte," "though a poem on such a theme could never be very important" (Carpenter, 109).

5. John Frederick Nims, "The Sestina," in *A Local Habitation: Essays on Poetry* (Ann Arbor: University of Michigan Press, 1985), 282.

6. See Wilmon Brewer, *Sonnets and Sestinas* (Boston: Cornhill Publishing Company, 1937), 203.

7. For discussions of the sestina's popularity, see John Hollander, *Rhyme's Reason: A Guide to English Verse*, enlarged ed. (New Haven: Yale University Press, 1989), 78–82; Paul Cummins, "The Sestina in the 20th Century," *Concerning Poetry* 11, no. 1 (spring 1978): 15–23; Neil Querengesser, "Attractions of the Contemporary Sestina," *English Studies in Canada* 18, no. 2 (June 1992): 199–213; and Miller Williams, *Patterns of Poetry: An Encyclopedia of Forms* (Baton Rouge: Louisiana State University Press, 1986), 93–100. I have also enjoyed the sensitive discussion of midcentury sestinas in Edward Brunner, "The Lure of the Sestina," in *Cold War Poetry* (Urbana: University of Illinois Press, 2001), 160–82. In contrast to Brunner, I date the crucial moment in the sestina's development a little earlier, stressing the influence of the literary and cultural politics of the Great Depression and New Criticism rather than that of the cold war.

8. In addition to the sestinas I have already cited and those I will specifically discuss, see W. H. Auden, "Have a Good Time," "Kairos and Logos," and "Sebastian," in *Collected Poems*, 68–69, 305–10, 419–20; Elizabeth Bishop, "Sestina," in *The Complete Poems, 1927–1979* (New York: Farrar, Straus and Giroux, 1980), 123–24; W. S. Merwin, "Variation on a Line by Emerson" and "Sestina," in *A Mask for Janus* (New Haven: Yale University Press, 1952), 34–35, 48–49; John Ashbery, "Poem," "The Painter," and "A Pastoral," in *Some Trees* (New York: Corinth Books, 1970), 24–25, 54–55, 72–73; Ashbery, "Farm Implements and Rutabagas in a Landscape," in *The Double Dream of Spring* (New York: E. P. Dutton and Company, 1970), 47–48; James Merrill, "Tomorrows," in *The Yellow Pages* (Cambridge, Mass.: Temple Bar Bookshop, 1974), 65–66; Anthony Hecht, "Sestina d'Inverno," in *Collected Earlier Poems* (New York: Alfred A. Knopf, 1990), 134–35; Donald Justice, "A Dream Sestina," "Sestina on Six Words by Weldon Kees," and "The Metamorphosis," in *The Summer Anniversaries* (Middletown, Conn.: Wesleyan University Press, 1960), 12–13, 14–15, 18–19; Marilyn Hacker, "An Alexandrite Pendant for My Mother," "Landscape for Insurrection," "Forage Sestina," "Sestina," "Nimue to Merlin," and "Untoward Occurrence at Embassy Poetry Reading," in *Presentation Piece* (New York: Viking Press, 1974), 10–11, 59–60, 67–68, 87–88, 97–98, 108–9; Hacker, "Towards Autumn" and "Inheritances," in *Selected Poems, 1965–1990* (New York: W. W. Norton, 1994), 139–40, 159–60; and Seamus Heaney, "Two Lorries," in *The Spirit Level* (London: Faber and Faber, 1996), 17–18. See also Agha Shahid Ali, "The Floating Post Office," in *The Country Without a Post Office* (New York: W. W. Norton, 1997), 52–3; Julia Alvarez, "Bilingual Sestina," in *A Formal Feeling Comes: Poems in Form by Contemporary Women*, ed., Annie Finch (Brownsville, Ore.: Story Line Press, 1994), 22–4; Amy Clampitt, "The Reedbeds of the Hackensack," in *The Collected Poems of Amy Clampitt* (New York: Alfred A. Knopf, 1997), 165–66; Mona Van Duyn, "Memoir," in *Near Changes* (New York: Alfred A. Knopf, 1990), 60–61; Weldon Kees, "After the Trial" and "Sestina: Travel Notes," in *The Collected Poems of Weldon Kees*, ed. Donald Justice, rev. ed. (Lincoln: University of Nebraska Press, 1975), 18–19, 63–64; Harry Matthews, "'Histoire,'" in *The Best American Poetry, 1988*, ed. John Ashbery (New York: Collier Books, 1988), 132–34; and David Lehman, "Operation Memory," in Ashbery, *Best American Poetry, 1988*, 106–7; Lehman, "The Thirty-nine Steps," in *An Alternative to*

Speech (Princeton, N.J.: Princeton University Press, 1986), 23–24. For bibliographies that include other sestinas, see Paul Cummins, "The Sestina in the 20th Century," 15–23; and John Frederick Nims, "The Sestina," 282.

9. See, for example, Diane Wakoski's "Sestina to the Common Glass of Beer: I Do Not Drink Beer," in *Strong Measures: Contemporary American Poetry in Traditional Forms*, ed. Philip Dacey and David Jauss (New York: Harper and Row, 1986), 389–90.

10. James E. B. Breslin, *From Modern to Contemporary: American Poetry, 1945–1965* (Chicago: University of Chicago Press, 1984), 38.

11. Louis Zukofsky, *All the Collected Short Poems, 1923–1964* (New York: W. W. Norton, 1971), 77.

12. Candace W. MacMahon, *Elizabeth Bishop: A Bibliography, 1927–1979* (Charlottesville: University Press of Virginia, 1980), 143.

13. W. H. Auden, *The Dyer's Hand and Other Essays* (New York: Random House, 1962), 47.

14. William Empson, *Seven Types of Ambiguity* (n.p.: New Directions, 1947), 2.

15. John Fuller, *W. H. Auden: A Commentary* (Princeton, N.J.: Princeton University Press, 1998), 154; William Empson, *Seven Types of Ambiguity*, 38.

16. Leslie A. Fiedler, "Dante: Green Thoughts in a Green Shade," in *No! In Thunder: Essays on Myth and Literature* (Boston: Beacon Press, 1960), 24.

17. In addition to the criticisms of the sestina that, in the course of this chapter, I will cite and specifically discuss, see Paul Fussell Jr., *Poetic Meter and Poetic Form*, rev. ed. (New York: Random House, 1979), 145; Philip Hobsbaum, *Metre, Rhythm and Verse Form* (London: Routledge, 1996), 172; Harvey Gross, *Sound and Form in Modern Poetry: A Study of Prosody from Thomas Hardy to Robert Lowell* (Ann Arbor: University of Michigan Press, 1973), 255; Robert Hillyer, *In Pursuit of Poetry* (New York: McGraw-Hill, 1960), 88; and Charles Bernstein, *A Poetics* (Cambridge, Mass.: Harvard University Press, 1992), 39. On the sestina's current lack of critical respect, see James Cummins, "Calliope Music: Notes on the Sestina," in *After New Formalism: Poets on Form, Narrative, and Tradition*, ed. Annie Finch (Ashland, Ore.: Story Line Press, 1999), 133–43.

18. Mark Rudman, *Diverse Voices: Essays on Poets and Poetry* (Brownsville, Ore.: Story Line Press, 1993), 201.

19. Peter Stitt, *Uncertainty and Plenitude: Five Contemporary Poets* (Iowa City: University of Iowa Press, 1997), 31.

20. Dana Gioia, "My Confessional Sestina," in *Rebel Angels: 25 Poets of the New Formalism*, ed. Mark Jarman and David Mason (Brownsville, Ore.: Story Line Press, 1996), 48–49; Edward Hirsch, "Nightsong: Ferris Wheel by the Sea," in *For the Sleepwalkers: Poems by Edward Hirsch* (New York: Alfred A. Knopf, 1981), 64–65; Alice Fulton, "You Can't Rhumboogie in a Ball and Chain," in *The Jazz Poetry Anthology*, ed. Sascha Feinstein and Yusef Komunyakaa (Bloomington: Indiana University Press, 1991), 63–64; Donald Hall, "Sestina," in *The Dark Houses* (New York: Viking Press, 1958), 47–48; and Alan Ansen, "A Fit of Something against Something," in *Contact Highs: Selected Poems, 1957–1987* (Elmwood Park, Ill.: Dalkey Archive Press, 1989), 17–18.

21. Eliot Weinberger's *American Poetry since 1950: Innovators and Outsiders* (New York: Marsilio, 1993) rather baldly expresses this notion. Weinberger states the postwar

generation's contribution to twentieth-century poetry: "Canonized early in their career, these poets formed an Establishment for a new avant-garde, the century's second great flowering, to lay siege to—much as Pound and the others had seen as their task the demolition of *fin de siècle* English poetry" (397). Less overtly polemical literary histories echo this position, albeit in a more restrained fashion. See Paul E. B. Breslin, *From Modern to Contemporary*; his entry on poetry from 1945 to the present; Breslin, *Columbia Literary History of the United States*, gen. ed. Emory Elliott (New York: Columbia University Press, 1988), s.v. "1945 to the Present: Poetry," 1079–1100; and Robert von Hallberg, "Rear Guards," in *The Cambridge History of American Literature*, ed. Sacvan Bercovitch, vol. 8, *Poetry and Criticism, 1940–1995* (New York: Cambridge University Press, 1996), 56–82. All three accounts offer lucid and, in many ways, compelling histories of postwar to contemporary poetry as a tale of the "rear guard" and the "avant guard," a story, however, that I wish to complicate.

22. Marjorie Perloff, *Poetry On & Off the Page: Essays for Emergent Occasions* (Evanston, Ill.: Northwestern University Press, 1998), xi; Amiri Baraka, *The Autobiography of LeRoi Jones* (New York: Freundlich Books, 1984), 158.

23. Anthony Hecht, *The Transparent Man* (New York: Alfred A. Knopf, 1990), 73.

24. Richard Wilbur, *New and Collected Poems* (San Diego: Harcourt, Brace and Company, 1988), 240.

25. Sigmund Freud, "The 'Uncanny,'" in *The Standard Edition of the Complete Psychological Works of Sigmund Freud*, ed. and trans. James Strachey, vol. 17, *An Infantile Neurosis and Other Works* (London: Hogarth Press, 1955), 234.

26. Anthony Hecht, "Sestina d'Inverno," in *Millions of Strange Shadows* (New York: Atheneum, 1977), 31.

27. Hecht is quoted in John Frederick Nims and David Mason, *Western Wind: An Introduction to Poetry*, 3rd ed. (New York: McGraw-Hill, 1992), 535; I am also indebted to the text for its translation of the epigraph. George Steiner, *Language and Silence: Essays on Language, Literature, and the Inhuman* (New York: Atheneum, 1967), ix, 5.

28. See Marianne Shapiro, *Hieroglyph of Time: The Petrarchan Sestina* (Minneapolis: University of Minnesota Press, 1980), 160–209.

29. See Anthony Hecht, *On the Laws of the Poetic Art* (Princeton, N.J.: Princeton University Press, 1995). I take the second phrase from Hecht's poem "Peripeteia," in *Millions of Strange Shadows*, 37

30. Robert Jay Lifton and Eric Markusen, *The Genocidal Mentality: Nazi Holocaust and Nuclear Threat* (New York: Basic Books, 1990), 234–35. The second ellipsis is in the original.

31. Of course I take this phrase from Theodor Adorno's pronouncement, "To write poetry after Auschwitz is barbaric." See Adorno, "Cultural Criticism and Society," in *Prisms*, trans. Samuel and Shierry Weber (Cambridge, Mass.: MIT Press, 1981), 34.

32. See Wilmon Brewer, "History of the Sestina," in *Sonnets and Sestinas*, 181–213, especially 189, 191.

33. Stan Sanvel Rubin and Judith Kitchen, "'The Underside of the Story': A Conversation with Rita Dove," in *The Post-Confessionals: Conversations with American Poets of the Eighties*, ed. Earl G. Ingersoll, Judith Kitchen, and Stan Sanvel Rubin (Rutherford, N.J.: Associated University Presses, 1989), 154–55.

34. Helen Vendler, "Identity Markers," in *Callalloo* 17, no. 2 (spring 1994): 387.

35. See Donald Justice, "Early Poems," in *Selected Poems* (New York: Atheneum, 1979), 46.

36. Donald Justice, *The Summer Anniversaries* (Middletown, Conn.: Wesleyan University Press, 1959), 16–17.

37. Justice, *Platonic Scripts*, 23.

38. *The Conquest of Everest*, produced with the cooperation and assistance of the Royal Geographic Society and the Alpine Club, filmed by Thomas Stobart, commentary written by Louis MacNeice (London: London Films, 1953).

39. Edmund Hillary, *Nothing Venture, Nothing Win* (London: Hodder and Stoughton, 1975), 165–66.

40. Robert Richman, ed., *The Direction of Poetry: An Anthology of Rhymed and Metered Verse Written in the English Language since 1975* (Boston: Houghton Mifflin Company, 1988), xv.

41. Richard Wilbur, "On Formalism, Translation, and Beloved Books of Childhood," *Black Warrior Review* 22, no. 2 (spring–summer 1996), 145.

42. Ezra Pound, *The Spirit of Romance* (Norfolk, Conn.: New Directions, 1952), 27.

43. See Philip Booth, "Syracuse Years: 1966–1970," in *Certain Solitudes: On the Poetry of Donald Justice*, ed. Dana Gioia and William Logan (Fayetteville: University of Arkansas Press, 1997), 145.

44. Donald Justice, interview by Dana Gioia, in ibid., 195–96.

45. Justice, *Platonic Scripts*, 24. See John Cage, author's note to "Diary: How to Improve the World (You Will Only Make Matters Worse)," in Weinberger, *American Poetry since 1950*, 136.

46. I take this description of Cage's composition process from Marjorie Perloff, ed., *The Dance of the Intellect: Studies in the Poetry of the Pound Tradition* (London: Cambridge University Press, 1996), 205.

47. John Cage, *Silence: Lectures and Writings* (Middletown, Conn.: Wesleyan University Press, 1961), 12.

Chapter 2

1. See the introduction to Aijaz Ahmad, ed., *Ghazals of Ghalib* (New York: Columbia University Press, 1971), vii–xxviii.

2. James T. Patterson, *Grand Expectations: The United States, 1945–1974* (New York: Oxford University Press, 1996), 682; Adrienne Rich, *Collected Early Poems, 1950–1970* (New York: W. W. Norton, 1993), 337–55, 368–72. See also Rich, "Late Ghazal," in *Dark Fields of the Republic: Poems, 1991–1995* (New York: W. W. Norton, 1995), 43.

3. Mirza Asadullah Khan Ghalib, "Ghazal," in *Ravishing DisUnities: Real Ghazals in English*, ed. Agha Shahid Ali, trans. Andrew McCord (Hanover, N.H.: University Press of New England, 2000), 62.

4. The one exception is that Rich's translations rather unavoidably mention the poet's pen name in the final couplet.

5. K. C. Kanda, *Masterpieces of the Urdu Ghazal: From the 17th to the 20th Century* (New Delhi: Sterling Publishers, 1994), 3.

6. Adrienne Rich, *Adrienne Rich's Poetry and Prose*, ed. Barbara Charlesworth Gelpi and Albert Gelpi (New York: W. W. Norton, 1993), 165.

7. See Ralph Russell and Khurshidul Islam, eds., *Ghalib, 1797–1869: Life and Letters* (Delhi: Oxford University Press, 1994), 91–93.

8. Imamu Amiri Baraka (LeRoi Jones), *Three Books by Imamu Amiri Baraka (LeRoi Jones)* (New York: Grove Press, 1975), 59.

9. Imamu Amiri Baraka (LeRoi Jones), *Black Magic: Collected Poetry, 1961–1967* (Indianapolis: Bobbs-Merrill Company, 1969), 116.

10. Baraka, *Three Books*, 63; Eldridge Cleaver, *Soul on Ice* (New York: McGraw-Hill, 1968), 14.

11. Jim Harrison, *Outlyer and Ghazals* (New York: Simon and Schuster, 1971), 26.

12. Hayden Carruth, *Selected Essays and Reviews* (Port Townsend, Wash.: Copper Canyon Press, 1996), 298.

13. See Angela Y. Davis, *Blues Legacies and Black Feminism: Gertrude "Ma" Rainey, Bessie Smith, and Billie Holiday* (New York: Pantheon, 1998), 211.

14. LeRoi Jones (Amiri Baraka), "The Changing Same (R&B and New Black Music)," in *The Black Aesthetic*, ed. Addison Gayle Jr. (Garden City, N.Y.: Doubleday and Company, 1971), 125, 121.

15. Samuel Charters, *The Poetry of the Blues* (New York: Oak Publications, 1963), 9.

16. Stephen Henderson, "Saturation: Progress Report on a Theory of Black Poetry," *Black World* 24, no. 7 (May 1975): 9–10.

17. Samuel Charters, *The Legacy of the Blues* (New York: Da Capo, 1977), 22.

18. John Thompson, *Stilt Jack* (Toronto: Anansi, 1978); Denise Levertov, *Oblique Prayers: New Poems with 14 Translations from Jean Joubert* (New York: New Directions, 1984), 6–7.

19. Agha Shahid Ali, "The Ghazal in America: May I?" in *After New Formalism: Poets on Form, Narrative, and Tradition*, ed. Annie Finch (Ashland, Ore.: Story Line Press, 1999), 123.

20. See also Agha Shahid Ali, "Ghazal: The Charms of a Considered Disunity," in *The Practice of Poetry: Writing Exercises from Poets Who Teach*, ed. Robin Behn and Chase Twitchell (New York: HarperCollins, 1992), 205–9; and Ali, "Ghazal: To Be Teased into DisUnity," in *An Exaltation of Forms: Contemporary Poets Celebrate the Diversity of Their Art*, ed. Annie Finch and Kathrine Varnes (Ann Arbor: University of Michigan Press, 2002), 210–16.

21. See Ali's description in his introduction to Faiz Akhmed Faiz, *The Rebel's Silhouette: Selected Poems*, trans. Agha Shahid Ali, rev. ed. (Amherst: University of Massachusetts Press, 1995), ix–xii.

22. Agha Shahid Ali, *In Memory of Begum Akhtar* (Calcutta: Writers Workshop, 1979), 16.

23. Agha Iqbal Ali and Hena Zafir Ahmad retitled the poem "By Exiles" for *Call Me Ishmael Tonight: A Book of Ghazals* (New York: W. W. Norton, 2003), 28–29. See also Agha Shahid Ali, "Ghazal I," *Triquarterly*, 100 (fall 1997): 24–25.

24. Edward Said, "The Mind of Winter: Reflections on Life in Exile," *Harper's* 269, no. 161 (September 1984): 51.

25. I take this phrase from Braj B. Kachru, *Kashmiri Literature*, vol. 8, fasc. 4 of *A History of Indian Literature*, ed. Jan Gonda (Wiesbaden, Germany: Otto Harrassowitz, 1981), 78. See also Ali's "Introducing," in *In Memory of Begum Akhtar*, 13.

26. Agha Shahid Ali, *Rooms Are Never Finished* (New York: W. W. Norton, 2002), 73.

27. See translator's introduction to *The Green Sea of Heaven: Fifty Ghazals from the Díwán of Háfiz*, trans. Elizabeth T. Gray Junior (Ashland, Ore.: White Cloud Press, 1995), quoted in Ghalib, *Ravishing DisUnities*, 4.

28. Debra Fried, "Rhyme Puns," in *On Puns: The Foundation of Letters*, ed. Jonathan Culler (Oxford: Basil Blackwell, 1988), 83.

29. See Karen W. Arenson, "Columbia Debates a Professor's 'Gesture,'" *New York Times*, October 19, 2000.

30. M. L. Williams, untitled essay, *Rattapallax* 7 (2002): 146. Williams was one of the principal organizers of the ghazal chain; my description of the writing of the poem draws from his account and the accounts of his fellow organizers Yerra Sugarman and Christopher Merrill, both contained in *Rattapallax* 7 (2002): 129–130 and 149–150, respectively.

Chapter 3

1. Umberto Eco, *Postscript to the Name of the Rose*, trans. William Weaver (San Diego: Harcourt Brace Jovanovich, 1983), 67.

2. Vivian Gornick, *The End of the Novel of Love* (Boston: Beacon Press, 1997), 165.

3. Quoted in *The Fifties* 1, no. 2 (1959), inside cover.

4. See Rafael Campo, "Imagining Drag," in *What the Body Told* (Durham, N.C.: Duke University Press, 1996), 34.

Among the many noteworthy sonnets left undiscussed here because of space constraints are those in J. D. McClatchy, *Ten Commandments* (New York: Alfred A. Knopf, 1998); Maureen Seaton, *Fear of Subways* (Portland, Ore.: Eighth Mountain Press, 1991); Seaton, *The Sea among the Cupboards* (Minneapolis: New Rivers Press, 1992); and Carl Phillips, envoi to "Cortège," in *Cortège* (St. Paul, Minn.: Graywolf Press, 1995), 28. For a fascinating use of what the author calls "the sexier aspect of the sonnet," its "[s]exual ambiguities" and themes of "Male Friendship and Love" (Anthony Hecht, "The Sonnet: Ruminations on Form, Sex, and History," *Antioch Review* 55, no. 2 (spring 1997): 140, 142), see Anthony Hecht, "The Feast of Stephen," in *Millions of Strange Shadows* (New York: Atheneum, 1977), 46–47.

5. Michael Cunningham, *The Hours* (New York: Farrar, Straus and Giroux, 1998), 203.

6. Mary Galvin, *Queer Poetics: Five Modernist Women Writers* (Westport, Conn.: Greenwood Press, 1999), xii; and Lynn Keller, *Forms of Expansion: Recent Long Poems by Women* (Chicago: University of Chicago Press, 1997), 158. In Keller's otherwise very astute reading of *Love, Death, and the Changing of the Seasons*, her praise remains tempered by her disinclination to believe that "regular, closed forms and unfragmented narratives may be adequate to the postmodern ear or to exploration of female difference" (185). On

this point, see also Joan Retallack's "Non-Euclidean Narrative Combustion (Or, What the Subtitles Can't Say)," in *Conversant Essays: Contemporary Poets on Poetry*, James McCorkle, ed. (Detroit: Wayne State University Press, 1990), 491–509.

7. Timothy Steele, *Missing Measures: Modern Poetry and the Revolt against Meter* (Fayetteville: University of Arkansas Press, 1990), 289–90. See also Denis Donoghue, "Teaching Literature: The Force of Form," *New Literary History* 30, no. 1 (winter 1999): 5–24; John Hollander, introduction to *The Best American Poetry, 1998*, ed. John Hollander (New York: Scribner Poetry, 1998), 15–22; and Marjorie Perloff, "Literary Literacy," *Chronicle of Higher Education* 43, no. 35 (May 9, 1997): B4(2).

8. Paul Oppenheimer, *The Birth of the Modern Mind: Self, Consciousness, and the Invention of the Sonnet* (New York: Oxford University Press, 1989), 3. As befitting such a grand claim, Oppenheimer's notion of "inwardness" as well as his dating of its development remains contested. See, for example, Katharine Eisaman Maus's *Inwardness and the Theater in the English Renaissance* (Chicago: University of Chicago Press, 1995), especially the introduction, for a lucid overview of contemporary scholarship's debates about "inwardness." In *The 'Inward' Language: Sonnets of Wyatt, Sidney, Shakespeare, Donne* (Chicago: University of Chicago Press, 1983), Anne Fry suggests that Renaissance sonnets show a distinctive interest in "what a modern writer would call the *inner life*" (27). Whether this concern manifests itself during the English Renaissance or earlier is less relevant to my argument than the more general point that sonnets have played a large role in Western literary-cultural conceptions of a particular kind of "*inner life*."

9. Leonard Forster, *The Icy Fire: Five Studies in European Petrarchism* (Cambridge: Cambridge University Press, 1969), 8.

10. A point Fuller, among others, overlooks. See John Fuller, introduction to *The Sonnet* (London: Methuen and Company, 1972), 39. "This [Sonnet 130] is not, as the critics seem to think, an anti-Petrarchan exercise," John Kerrigan comments in his introduction to William Shakespeare, *The Sonnets and A Lover's Complaint*, ed. John Kerrigan (New York: Viking, 1986), 22. See also Forster, *Icy Fire*, 56–57.

11. Lawrence Stone, *The Family, Sex, and Marriage in England, 1500–1800* (London: Weidenfield and Nicolson, 1977), 284.

12. Peter Gay, *The Bourgeois Experience Victoria to Freud*, vol. 2, *The Tender Passion* (Oxford: Oxford University Press, 1986), 137.

13. W. B. Yeats, *Essays and Introductions* (New York: Collier Books, 1961), 497.

14. See Helen Vendler, *The Art of Shakespeare's Sonnets* (Cambridge, Mass.: Harvard University Press, 1997), 8–10.

15. Despite its polemics against contemporary free verse, Timothy Steele's *Missing Measures: Modern Poetry and the Revolt against Meter* contains the fullest treatment of this issue. See especially its opening chapter, "Poetry and Precedent: The Modern Movement and Free Verse," 29–68.

16. T. E. Hulme, *Further Speculations*, ed. Sam Hynes (Minneapolis: University of Minnesota Press, 1955), 74.

17. T. S. Eliot, *On Poetry and Poets* (New York: Farrar, Straus and Cudahy, 1957), 181; and Eliot, *Selected Prose of T. S. Eliot*, ed. Frank Kermode (New York: Harcourt Brace Jovanovich, 1975), 36.

18. William Carlos Williams, "The Tortuous Straightness of Chas. Henri Ford," in *Selected Essays of William Carlos Williams* (New York: Random House, 1954), 235–36; for another of Williams's more memorable condemnations of the sonnet, see *The Collected Later Poems of William Carlos Williams* (New York: New Directions, 1963), 5, where he comments, "To me all sonnets say the same thing of no importance."

19. Margaret Homans, "'Syllables of Velvet': Dickinson, Rossetti, and the Rhetorics of Sexuality," *Feminist Studies* 11, no. 3 (fall 1985): 570–93.

20. Michael R. G. Spiller, *The Sonnet Sequence: A Study of Its Strategies* (New York: Twayne Publishers, 1997), 8. Ironically, Spiller's fine work in the field, especially in *The Development of the Sonnet: An Introduction* (London: Routledge, 1992), offers ample evidence to contradict this statement.

21. See Stuart Curran, *Poetic Form and British Romanticism* (Oxford: Oxford University Press, 1986), 29–55. For specific numbers, see Enid Hamer, *The English Sonnet: An Anthology* (London: Methuen and Company, 1936), xxix–xxxv.

22. Samuel Johnson, *Johnson's Dictionary: A Modern Selection*, ed. E. L. McAdam and George Milne (New York: Modern Library, 1965), 389.

23. Quoted in Hallett Smith, *The Tension of the Lyre: Poetry in Shakespeare's Sonnets* (San Marino, Calif.: Huntington Library, 1981), 144.

24. Kate Light, *The Laws of Falling Bodies* (Brownsville, Ore.: Story Line Press, 1997), 4.

25. Seamus Heaney, *Field Work* (New York: Farrar, Straus and Giroux, 1979), 42.

26. Irving Singer, *The Nature of Love*, vol. 2, *Courtly and Romantic* (Chicago: University of Chicago Press, 1987), 6

27. William Butler Yeats, *The Collected Poems of W. B. Yeats*, ed. Richard J. Finneran (New York: Scribner, 1989), 81.

28. Quoted from a January 21, 1964, conversation in Robert Craft, *Stravinsky: Chronicle of a Friendship*, rev. ed. (Nashville: Vanderbilt University Press, 1994), 392. See also W. H. Auden, "Shakespeare's Sonnets," in *Forewords and Afterwords*, ed. Edward Mendelson (New York: Random House, 1973), 88–108.

29. Joseph Pequigney, *Such is My Love: A Study of Shakespeare's Sonnets* (Chicago: University of Chicago Press, 1985), 1; Eve Kosofsky Sedgwick, *Between Men: English Literature and Male Homosocial Desire* (New York: Columbia University Press, 1985).

30. See Jonathan Goldberg, ed., *Queering the Renaissance* (Durham, N.C.: Duke University Press, 1994), especially Goldberg's introduction, which offers an overview of Sedgwick's influence on the field.

31. John Crowe Ransom, *The World's Body* (Baton Rouge: Louisiana State University Press, 1968), 385.

32. See Casey Charles, "Was Shakespeare Gay?: Sonnet 20 and the Politics of Pedagogy," *College Literature* 25, no. 3 (fall 1998): 35–51, which counsels teachers on how to respond when students raise this seemingly inevitable question.

33. See Gertrude Stein, "A Sonnet," from "Patriarchal Poetry," in *The Yale Gertrude Stein*, ed. Richard Kostelanetz (New Haven: Yale University Press, 1980), 124, which parodies the sonnet's conventions; and Adrienne Rich, "Love Poem," in *Time's Power:*

Poems, 1985–1988 (New York: W. W. Norton, 1989), 7, which declares "to write for you / a pretty sonnet / would be untrue."

34. Samuel Taylor Coleridge, *The Collected Works of Samuel Taylor Coleridge*, ed. George Whalley, vol. 12, *Marginalia I* (Princeton, N.J.: Princeton University Press, 1980), 43.

35. For a sense of Marilyn Hacker's reading in and appreciation of queer theory, see her review in *Nation* 257, no. 22 (December 27, 1993): 810. Among the books Hacker recommends are Eve Kosofsky Sedgwick's *Tendencies* (calling Sedgwick "one of the smartest and wittiest critics writing") and Terry Castle's *The Apparitional Lesbian*.

36. Rafael Campo, *The Poetry of Healing: A Doctor's Education in Empathy, Identity, and Desire* (New York: W. W. Norton, 1997), 94, 95, 97–98.

37. See Tony Harrison, *Selected Poems* (London: Penguin Books, 1984), 112–249.

38. Campo, *The Desire to Heal*, 194–95.

39. For the two iconic statements of these positions, see Robert Bly, "Looking for Dragon Smoke," in *Naked Poetry: Recent American Poetry in Open Forms*, ed. Stephen Berg and Robert Mezey (New York: Bobbs-Merrill Company, 1969), 161–64; and Ezra Pound, "A Retrospect," in *Literary Essays of Ezra Pound* (New York: New Directions, 1968), 3–14.

40. For examples of this other, less productive line of argument, see Brad Leithauser, "The Confinement of Free Verse," in McCorkle, *Conversant Essays*, 162–74; and Frederick Turner and Ernst Pöppel, "The Neural Lyre: Poetic Meter, the Brain, and Time," *in New Expansive Poetry: Theory, Criticism, History*, ed. R. S. Gwynn (Ashland, Ore.: Story Line Press, 1999), 86–119.

41. Henri Cole, *The Visible Man* (New York: Alfred A. Knopf, 1998), 46.

42. See James Brooke, "Gay Man Beaten and Left for Dead: Two Are Charged," *New York Times*, October 10, 1998.

43. Marilyn Hacker, *Love, Death, and the Changing of the Seasons* (New York: Arbor House, 1986), 212.

44. Several critics of Hacker's work express distaste for her enjambments because they are so regular. See, for example, Kevin Walzer, *The Ghost of Tradition: Expansive Poetry and Postmodernism* (Ashland, Ore.: Story Line Press, 1998), where Walzer cites this sonnet as exemplifying Hacker's technical deficiencies: "This poem's rough linebreaks ('make / you,' 'dead / chances')," Walzer comments, "indicate the form mastering the poet, rather than vice versa" (9).

45. John Hollander, "'Sense Variously Drawn Out': On English Enjambment," in *Vision and Resonance: Two Senses of Poetic Form*, 2d ed. (New Haven: Yale University Press, 1985), 106.

46. Justus George Lawler, *Celestial Pantomime: Poetic Structures of Transcendence* (New Haven: Yale University Press, 1979), 84.

47. Shakespeare, *Sonnets and A Lover's Complaint*, 147.

48. John Weir, "Marilyn Hacker," *Advocate*, September 20, 1994, 54.

49. Quoted in Spiller, *The Development of the Sonnet*, 190.

50. Marilyn Hacker, "Meditating Formally," in *A Formal Feeling Comes: Poems in Form by Contemporary Women*, ed. Annie Finch (Brownsville, Ore.: Story Line Press, 1994), 87.

Chapter 4

1. Eavan Boland, "The Death of Reason," in *In a Time of Violence* (Manchester, England: Carcaret, 1994), 9–10.

2. Stephen Dobyns, *Best Words, Best Order: Essays on Poetry* (New York: St. Martin's Press, 1996), 56–57.

3. Mark Strand and Eavan Boland, eds., *The Making of a Poem: A Norton Anthology of Poetic Forms* (New York: W. W. Norton, 2000), 122–23. See this chapter's first footnote for a more extensive consideration of the anthology and the view of eighteenth-century culture and literature that it expresses.

4. Roy Porter, *English Society in the Eighteenth Century* (New York: Penguin Books, 1982), 113–14, 118.

5. Alexander Pope, *The Poems of Alexander Pope*, ed. John Butt (New Haven: Yale University Press, 1963), 800.

6. Margaret Doody, *The Daring Muse: Augustan Poetry Reconsidered* (Cambridge: Cambridge University Press, 1985), 236–37.

7. The clearest example of this tendency is Doody's explanation of the heroic couplet's popularity: "One might say that the Augustans had binary minds, that they thought in twos. Presumably a series of historical events involving, first, a Civil War (between two chief sides) and then a series of political disputes (involving the same two sides as two national parties historically modified) all leading, however reluctantly, to the evolution of what we now know as the two-party system had something to do with this cast of thought" (*Daring Muse*, 233).

8. Predating the first creative-writing program, the debate over this discipline is long and contentious. Recently, following Joseph Epstein, Dana Gioia and Bruce Bawer blame creative-writing programs for poetry's increasing cultural marginalization, but do so at the risk of mistaking "effects for causes," as Alan Shapiro notes in *In Praise of the Impure: Poetry and the Ethical Imagination: Essays, 1980–1991* (Evanston, Ill.: Northwestern University Press, 1993), 5. However, like Gioia, I share Shapiro's fear that "our MFA programs . . . ghettoize the creative writers from the scholars and critics" (Gioia, *Can Poetry Matter? Essays on Poetry and American Culture* [St. Paul, Minn.: Graywolf Press, 1992], 178) and overly emphasize contemporary literature; some of my arguments later in this essay will additionally echo Marjorie Perloff's criticisms of the institutional divisions between creative writing's "formalism" and literary studies' occasionally fierce hostility to aesthetics. See, for example, Marjorie Perloff, *Poetic License: Essays on Modernist and Postmodernist Lyric* (Evanston, Ill.: Northwestern University Press, 1990), 229–30. For classic defenses of the creative-writing discipline, see Wallace Stegner, *On the Teaching of Creative Writing: Responses to a Series of Questions*, ed. Edward Connery Lathem (Hanover, N.H.: University Press of New England, 1988); Dave Smith, "Notes on Responsibility and the Teaching of Creative Writing," in *Local Assays: On Contemporary American Poetry* (Urbana: University of Illinois Press, 1985), 215–28; and Richard Hugo, "In Defense of Creative-Writing Classes," in *The Triggering Town: Lectures and Essays on Poetry and Writing* (New York: W. W. Norton, 1977), 53–66. "Poetry and the University," Bruce Bawer's less-than-judicious attack on the creative-writing discipline, can be found in *Poetry after Modernism*, ed. Robert McDowell (Brownsville, Ore.: Story Line Press, 1991).

9. David Lehman, ed., *Ecstatic Occasions, Expedient Forms: 85 Leading Contemporary Poets Select and Comment on Their Poems*, 2d ed. (Ann Arbor: University of Michigan Press, 1996). See also Philip Dacey and David Jauss, eds., *Strong Measures: Contemporary American Poetry in Traditional Forms* (New York: Harper and Row, 1986); Robert Richman, ed., *The Direction of Poetry: An Anthology of Rhymed and Metered Verse Written in the English Language since 1975* (Boston: Houghton Mifflin, 1988); and Annie Finch, ed., *A Formal Feeling Comes: Poems in Form by Contemporary Women* (Brownsville, Ore.: Story Line Press, 1994), recent anthologies that are organized according to verse forms and feature a similar lack of heroic couplets. For example, the 380-page *A Formal Feeling Comes* contains only two poems in heroic couplets, as opposed to five sestinas, six villanelles, and thirty-one sonnets. Mark Jarman and David Mason, eds., *Rebel Angels: 25 Poets of the New Formalism* (Brownsville, Ore.: Story Line Press, 1996) offers an exception to this pattern, with more poems in heroic couplets than sestinas, villanelles, or sonnets. However, this anthology reveals more about the editors' preferences than a more general trend. As will be clear from the contemporary examples of heroic couplets that I will cite and analyze, the heroic couplet currently is not a wholly unused form but a neglected one.

Much more common is the view that guides Mark Strand and Eavan Boland's organization of *The Making of a Poem*, 122: "This [the heroic couplet] is one of the few forms that we have not annotated with a contemporary context. We mean this section to be almost a small laboratory to show how a single, unassuming form could suddenly rise to express the grander hopes of a time." Indeed, Strand and Boland link the couplet so strongly to "the Augustan Age" that they cannot imagine how it fits the "contemporary context." Accordingly, they include only one heroic couplet poem written during the last fifty years and only two written during the last century, a remarkable decision considering the emphasis on contemporary examples that guides their considerations of other forms. More than half of the sonnets they present in their section on that form were written during the last century and more than a quarter written during the last fifty years. In a telling contrast to their discussion of the couplet, they include a consideration of the sonnet's "contemporary context," which argues for the form's continued relevance, and go so far as to call the form "a perfect vehicle for twentieth-century poets." See *The Making of a Poem*, 58–59, 71–72, 122.

10. J. M. Coetzee, *Elizabeth Costello* (New York: Viking, 2003), 127.

11. For example, see Dana Gioia, "Notes on the New Formalism," in *Can Poetry Matter?* 40.

12. John Berryman, *Collected Poems, 1937–1971*, ed. Charles Thornbury (New York: Farrar, Straus and Giroux, 1989), 51.

13. Thom Gunn, *The Man with Night Sweats* (London: Faber and Faber, 1992), 61.

14. William Bowman Piper, *The Heroic Couplet* (Cleveland: Press of Case Western University, 1969), 23–24.

15. Alastair Fowler, *The Country House Poem: A Cabinet of Seventeenth-Century Estate Poems and Related Items* (Edinburgh: Edinburgh University Press, 1994), 15.

16. Derek Mahon, *The Yaddo Letter* (Loughcrew: Gallery Books, 1995), 27.

17. Derek Walcott, *Collected Poems, 1948–1984* (New York: Farrar, Straus and Giroux, 1986), 407.

18. James Longenbach, "Ashbery and the Individual Talent," *American Literary History* 9, no. 1 (1997): 108. In *Modern Poetry after Modernism* (New York: Oxford University Press, 1997), Longenbach expands his argument with additional readings of other late-twentieth-century poets.

19. T. S. Eliot, *Collected Poems, 1909–1962* (New York: Harcourt, Brace and World, 1963), 190.

20. Harold Bloom, *The Western Canon: The Books and School of the Ages* (New York: Harcourt, Brace and Company, 1994), 11.

21. T. S. Eliot, *Selected Essays, 1917–1932* (New York: Harcourt, Brace and Company, 1932), 5.

22. Robert Hass, *Twentieth Century Pleasures: Prose on Poetry* (New York: Ecco Press, 1984), 70.

23. Wyatt Prunty, *"Fallen from the Symboled World": Precedents for the New Formalism* (New York: Oxford University Press, 1990), 57–88; Charles Altieri, *Self and Sensibility in Contemporary American Poetry* (Cambridge: Cambridge University Press, 1984), 22; Mary Kinzie, *The Cure of Poetry in an Age of Prose: Moral Essays on the Poet's Calling* (Chicago: University of Chicago Press, 1993), 1–26; and Donald Hall, *Poetry and Ambition: Essays, 1982–1988* (Ann Arbor: University of Michigan Press, 1988), 12–13.

24. Derek Walcott, *"Dream on Monkey Mountain" and Other Plays* (New York: Farrar, Straus and Giroux, 1970), 8, 9.

25. William Baer, ed., *Conversations with Derek Walcott* (Jackson: University Press of Mississippi, 1996), 62.

26. See John Gery, "Walcott's Spoiler and Spoiler's Walcott: The Commonwealth of Caiso," (lecture, Twentieth-Century Literature Conference, University of Louisville, 1998), which first brought to my attention Walcott's allusion to "Bedbug."

Chapter 5

1. See X. J. Kennedy and Dorothy Kennedy, "Last Ditch," *Counter / Measures*, no. 3 (1974): 216.

2. Unsigned, "Last Ditch," *Counter / Measures*, no. 2 (1973): 213.

3. Unsigned, "Coming in the Next *Counter / Measures*," *Counter / Measures*, no. 1 (1972): 116

4. Richman, *The Direction of Poetry*, xiii.

5. Unsigned, "Last Ditch," 213.

6. Tellingly, the same issue also favorably reviewed Ginsberg's recording of Blake's "Songs of Innocence and Experience." See X. J. Kennedy, "Piping down the Valleys Wild," *Counter / Measures*, no. 1 (1972): 98.

7. Rosmarie Waldrop, "I Can't Keep up with You," *Counter / Measures*, no. 1 (1972): 84.

8. Langston Hughes, *Shakespeare in Harlem* (New York: Alfred A. Knopf, 1945), unnumbered preface.

9. See, for instance, Alan Bold's otherwise very engaging introduction to *The Ballad* (London: Methuen and Company, 1979), which refers only in passing to the black folk

poetry tradition but makes no mention of black literary balladeers such Hughes, Cullen, and Brooks.

10. R. Murray Schafer, *The Tuning of the World: Toward a Theory of Soundscape Design* (Philadelphia: University of Pennsylvania Press, 1980), 274–75, 3–4.

11. See, for instance, Emily Ann Thompson, *The Soundscape of Modernity: Architectural Acoustics and the Culture of Listening in America, 1900–1933* (Cambridge, Mass.: MIT Press, 2002); Garret Stewart, *Reading Voices: Literature and the Phonotext* (Berkeley: University of California Press, 1990); and John Picker, *Victorian Soundscapes* (Oxford: Oxford University Press, 2003). I am especially indebted to the literature review that *Victorian Soundscapes* provides in its introduction.

Investigations of contemporary soundscapes' relation to poetry almost always ignore contemporary metrical verse to focus on "innovative poetics." See, for instance, the otherwise very interesting essays in Adalaide Morris, ed., *Sound States: Innovative Poetics and Acoustical Technologies* (Chapel Hill: University of North Carolina Press, 1997); and Charles Bernstein, ed., *Close Listening: Poetry and the Performed Word* (Oxford: Oxford University Press, 1998).

12. See Tracie Morris, "Hip-Hop Rhyme Formations: Open Your Ears," in *An Exaltation of Forms: Contemporary Poets Celebrate the Diversity of Their Art*, ed. Annie Finch and Kathrine Varnes (Ann Arbor: University of Michigan Press, 2002), 226–27. For a weird and somewhat disturbing self-examination of rap music's relation to a poet's particular work, see Geoffrey Hill's address to "RAPMASTER," the "evil twin," in *Speech! Speech!* (Washington, D.C.: Counterpoint, 2000), 46–48.

13. Derek Attridge, *Poetic Rhythm: An Introduction* (Cambridge: Cambridge University Press, 1995), 19.

14. Mark W. Booth, *The Experience of Songs* (New Haven: Yale University Press, 1981), 66–73, where he quotes Julian Jaynes's summary of the experiments I mention.

15. Reuven Tsur, for instance, cautions: "We have no access to what happens in that black box, the reader's head; we have only access to vocal performances." See Reuven Tsur, "Poetic Rhythm: Structure and Performance: An Empirical Study in Cognitive Poetics," 1987, available at www.tau.ac.il/~tsurxx/Synposis.html.

16. See Walter Jackson Bate, *John Keats* (Cambridge, Mass.: Harvard University Press, 1963), 416.

17. X. J. Kennedy, *Cross Ties: Selected Poems* (Athens: University of Georgia Press, 1985), 23.

18. X. J. Kennedy, commentary on "In a Prominent Bar in Secaucus One Day," in *Poet's Choice*, ed. Paul Engle and Joseph Langland (New York: Dial Press, 1962), 286.

19. William Wordsworth, *The Prose Works of William Wordsworth*, ed. W. J. B. Owen and Jane Worthington Smyser, vol. 3 (Oxford: Clarendon Press, 1974), 78.

20. Thomas Percy, *Reliques of Ancient English Poetry*, ed. J. V. Prichard (London: George Bell and Sons, 1876), 1:xii.

21. T. V. F. Brogan, *The New Princeton Encyclopedia of Poetry and Poetics*, ed. Alex Preminger and T. V. F. Brogan. (Princeton, N.J.: Princeton University Press, 1993), s.v. "ballad meter."

22. Antony Easthope, *Poetry as Discourse* (London: Methuen and Company, 1983), 77.

23. Colson Whitehead, *John Henry Days* (New York: Doubleday, 2001), 341.

24. Dudley Randall, ed., *The Black Poets* (New York: Bantam Books, 1971), xxiv.

25. James D. Sullivan, *On the Walls and in the Streets: American Poetry Broadsides from the 1960s* (Urbana: University of Illinois Press, 1997), 32.

26. Dana Gioia, *Interrogations at Noon* (St. Paul, Minn.: Graywolf Press, 2001), 66–67.

27. John Stuart Mill, "What is Poetry?" (1833), reprinted in Hazard Adams, ed., *Critical Theory since Plato* (New York: Harcourt Brace Jovanovich, 1971), 539.

28. R. S. Gwynn, *The Dark Horse* 9/10 (summer 2000): 83.

29. Marilyn Nelson Waniek, *The Homeplace: Poems by Marilyn Nelson Waniek* (Baton Rouge: Louisiana State University Press, 1990), 5. Nelson published *The Homeplace* under the name "Marilyn Nelson Waniek"; she has since returned to using the name "Marilyn Nelson." To avoid confusion, I refer to her as "Marilyn Nelson."

30. Susan Stewart, *Poetry and the Fate of the Senses* (Chicago: University of Chicago Press, 2002), 121.

31. See the "Experiments" that Bernstein posted on his Web site at http://epc.buffalo. edu/authors/bernstein/experiments.html (accessed 7 June 2004).

32. Charles Bernstein, *Republics of Reality, 1975–1995* (Los Angeles: Sun and Moon Press, 2000), 360.

33. Charles Bernstein, "Comedy and the Poetics of Political Form," in *The Politics of Poetic Form: Poetry and Public Policy*, ed. Charles Bernstein (New York: Roof Books, 1990), 237.

34. See W. H. Auden, ed., *The Oxford Book of Light Verse* (Oxford: Oxford University Press, 1945), 262–63, 396–98.

35. Charles Bernstein, *My Way: Speeches and Poems* (Chicago: University of Chicago Press, 1999), 10.

36. I take this phrase from Charles O. Hartman, "Syntax as Prosody" (lecture, Exploring Form and Narrative Conference, West Chester University, West Chester, Pa., June 2002).

37. Quoted in Nancy Williard, ed., *Angel in the Parlor: 5 Stories and 8 Essays* (New York: Harcourt Brace Jovanovich, 1983), 261.

38. Iona and Peter Opie, *The Oxford Nursery Rhyme Book* (New York: Oxford University Press, 1991), 36.

39. George Lyman Kittredge, introduction to *English and Scottish Popular Ballads*, ed. Helen Child Sargent and George Lyman Kittredge (Boston: Houghton Mifflin Company, 1932), xx.

40. Elizabeth Bishop, *The Complete Poems, 1927–1979* (New York: Farrar, Straus and Giroux, 1983), 133.

41. Donald Justice, *A Donald Justice Reader: Selected Poetry and Prose* (Hanover, N.H.: Middlebury College Press / University Press of New England, 1991), 77.

Conclusion

1. Oppen revises phrases from poems that appeared in two of Levine's books: "Grandmother in Heaven," in *1933: Poems by Philip Levine* (New York: Atheneum,

1974), 5; and "They Feed They Lion," in *They Feed They Lion* (New York: Atheneum, 1976), 34.

2. Robert Duncan, *Ground Work: Before the War* (New York: New Directions, 1984), 69

3. My reading is indebted to Michael Davidson's fine consideration of the sequence in *Ghostlier Demarcations: Modern Poetry and the Material World* (Berkeley: University of California Press, 1997), 181–90.

4. See Annie Finch, ed., *After New Formalism: Poets on Form, Narrative, and Tradition* (Ashland, Ore.: Story Line Press, 1999); and Anders Lundgerg, Jonas (J) Magnusson, and Jesper Olsson, eds., "After Language: 10 Statements," *OEI* 7–8 (2001), available at http://www.ubu.com/papers/oei/index.html.

5. See Williamson's essay, "Forms of Disguise," in the symposium "Poets on Form" organized by the Poetry Society of America and available at http://www.poetrysociety.org/journal/articles/ponform99.html.

6. H. L. Hix, *Rational Numbers: Poems by H. L. Hix* (Kirksville, Mo.: Truman State University Press, 2000), 20.

7. Olivia and Jack Solomon, eds., *"Honey in the Rock": The Ruby Pickens Tartt Collection of Religious Folk Songs from Sumter County, Alabama* (Macon, Ga.: Mercer University Press, 1991), 127.

8. *"Honey in the Rock,"* for instance, includes versions of "Let It Shine" and "Free at Last."

9. H. L Hix, *As Easy as Lying: Essays on Poetry* (Silver Springs, Md.: Etruscan Press, 2002), 50.

10. H. L. Hix, *Spirits Hovering over the Ashes: Legacies of Postmodern Theory* (Albany: State University of New York Press, 1995), 9.

11. Jennifer Moxley, *The Sense Record and Other Poems* (Washington, D.C.: Edge Books, 2002), 5–6.

12. For clarity's sake, I use the title that Perelman used in subsequent publications of the poem.

13. Peter Nicholls, "A Conversation with Bob Perelman," *Textual Practice* 12, no. 3 (1998): 530–32.

14. Quoted in Tom Sharp, "George Oppen, *Discrete Series*, 1929–1934," in *George Oppen, Man and Poet*, ed. Burton Hatlen (Orono, Me.: National Poetry Foundation, 1981), 275–76.

15. I refer of course to Pound's famous declaration, "To break the pentameter, that was the first heave," in *The Cantos of Ezra Pound* (New York: New Directions, 1970), 518.

16. With some reservations I take the term "bacchic" from classical prosody, where it refers to the arrangement of short and long syllables, not accented and unaccented syllables. The term's obscurity, though, helpfully suggests the oddness of the line's meter.

17. Ron Silliman's blog, Monday, December 9, 2002, available at http://ronsilliman.blogspot.com/2002_12.

18. Moxley comments that "as a set of theories about writing Language poetry ceased being of any help to me about 1989." Moxley's letter, in Lundgerg, Magnusson, and Olsson, "After Language," *OEI* 7–8 (2001), is available at http://www.ubu.com/papers/oei/moxley.html.

19. Peter Gizzi, "From a Field Glass," in *Artificial Heart* (Providence: Burning Deck Press, 1998), 45.

20. See Moxley's letter, in "After Language."

21. Marjorie Perloff and Robert von Hallberg, "Dialogue on Evaluation in Poetry," in *Professions: Conversations on the Future of Literary and Cultural Studies,* ed. Donald Hall (Urbana: University of Illinois Press, 2001), 87–108, available at http://epc.buffalo.edu/authors/perloff/articles/dialogue.html.

INDEX

"About Sonnets of Love; Some"
(Light), 68–69
African-American literature, 12–13,
51–52, 107, 111–12, 115
Afro-Caribbean literature, 100, 103–4
Agha, Shahid Ali, 14–15, 53–59
AIDS crisis, 63, 74–77, 93–96
Aijaz Ahmad, 43
Ali, Agha Shahid. See Agha, Shahid
Ali
amazon.com, poetry
recommendations on, 5
"American Sonnet" (Collins), 10
"Ananias, Ananias" (folk song), 129
Arnold, Matthew, 92
"Arte Povera" (Cole), 78
Ashbery, John, 16, 20
Attridge, Derek, 108
Auden, W. H., 19–24, 38, 71
Augustan Age, 67–68, 88–92
"Aunt Annie's Prayer" (Nelson), 119

Baker, Houston A., Jr., 13
"Ballad of Aunt Geneva, The"
(Nelson), 113, 115–20, 122

"Ballad of Birmingham" (Randall),
112–13
ballads, 6, 15, 105–25; performance
and, 108–11, 120, 125;
soundscapes and, 107–8;
structure of, 110, 113–15, 118,
122–24; Poems discussed: "Aunt
Annie's Prayer" (Nelson),
119; "The Ballad of Aunt
Geneva" (Nelson), 113, 115–20,
122; "Ballad of Birmingham"
(Randall), 112–13; "Dana
Gioia" (Gwynn), 115; "The
Death of Reason" (Boland),
87–88; "I Can't Keep up with
You" (Waldrop), 106–7; "In a
Prominent Bar in Secaucus
One Day" (Kennedy), 109;
"Rivulets of the Dead Jew"
(Bernstein), 120–25; "Summer
Storm" (Gioia), 113–15, 117, 120
Baraka, Imamu Amiri, 46–49, 51–52
Barnes, Barnabe, 19
"Baroque Wall-Fountain in Villa
Sciarra, A" (Wilbur), 78

"Batter my heart, three-personed God" (Donne), 79
"Bedbug" (Phillip), 104
Bernstein, Charles, 5, 10, 15, 120–25
Berryman, John, 92
Bishop, Elizabeth, 14, 17–25, 124
Black Aesthetic movement, 47, 52
Black Nationalism/Power movements, 14, 47, 49–50
blank verse, 7, 78–80, 134–35
Blasing, Konuk, 141n.17
Bloom, Harold, 101
"Blue Ghazals, The" (Rich), 43–44, 47–49
blues form, 13, 51–52, 106
Bly, Robert, 62
Boland, Eavan, 87–89, 93
Bold, Alan, 154n.9
"Book of Yolek, The" (Hecht), 25–32, 34
Booth, Mark W., 109–10
Borges, Jorge Luis, 5
Breslin, James E. B., 20
Brogan, T. V. F., 110
"Broken Ghazals" (Levertov), 53
Brooks, Garth, 91
Brooks, Gwendolyn, 11, 12, 107
Bruner, Simeon, 6, 7–8
Brunner, Edward, 143n.7

Cage, John, 9, 39–41
Calypso rhythms, 104
Campo, Rafael, 15, 63, 72–77, 80
Carew, Thomas, 96–97
Carruth, Hayden, 51–52
Cartland, Barbara, 61
centos, 16
Changing Light at Sandover, The (Merrill), 93
Charters, Samuel, 52
Child, F. J., 110
Churchill, Winston, 11
Cleaver, Eldridge, 47, 50

closed verse forms, 10, 16
Cochran, Johnnie, 91
Coetzee, J. M., 91
Cole, Henri, 15, 63, 77–80
Coleridge, Samuel Taylor, 72, 92, 110
Collins, Billy, 10–11
common meter, 110, 123
confessional lyrics, 107
"Confession" (Perelman), 132
"Conquest of Everest, The" (BBC documentary), 35–36, 41
Corless-Smith, Martin, 8
Counter / Measures, 105–7
"Counting the Mad" (Justice), 124
"Countin' the Blues" (Rainey), 51
country house poetry, 96
creative writers, criticism by, 9, 15, 90
Creeley, Robert, 88
Cullen, Countee, 13
Cunningham, J. V., 105
Cunningham, Michael, 63

Dacey, Philip, 37
"Dana Gioia" (Gwynn), 115
Daniel, Arnaut, 19
Dante Alighieri, 19, 23, 29, 32, 65
"Death of Reason, The" (Boland), 87–88
Dickinson, Emily, 67
Dobyns, Stephen, 88–90, 95
Donne, John, 79, 85
Donoghue, Denis, 63
Doody, Margaret Anne, 89–90, 93, 95
Dove, Rita, 33, 115
Dryden, John, 92
Duncan, Robert, 127

Easthope, Antony, 3, 111
Eco, Umberto, 61–62
eighteenth-century literature, 65, 67–68, 88–92
Eliot, T. S., 7, 20, 66, 100, 101

Empson, William, 21–22
enjambments, 9, 75–76, 81–84,
     96–98, 133
exile, politics of, 47, 53, 55–57
experimental forms, 9–10,
     15–16, 120, 141n.17. *See also*
     L=A=N=G=U=A=G=E Writing

feminist criticism, 66–69
Fiedler, Leslie, 23
Forster, Leonard, 65, 79
free verse, 7, 11, 20, 37, 53, 77, 88, 99,
     101–3
Freud, Sigmund, 27–28
Fried, Debra, 57
From the Other Side of the Century,
     127
Frost, Robert, 11
Fuller, John, 22, 149n.10
Fussell, Paul, 3

"Garden. A Theophany of ECCO
     HOME a dialectical lyric, The"
     (Corless-Smith), 8
Gay, Peter, 66
Ghalib, Mirza, 43–46
"Ghazal" (Ghalib), 44–45
"Ghazal" (Haag), 58
"Ghazal I" (Agha), 53–57
ghazals, 6, 14–15, 43–60, 111; history
     of, 43–44; structure of, 44–45, 49,
     53, 55–57, 59; *Poems discussed:*
     "The Blue Ghazals" (Rich),
     43–44, 47–49; "Broken Ghazals"
     (Levertov), 53; "Ghazal for
     Shahid (Missing You in Palm
     Springs, 2001)", 58–59; "Ghazal"
     (Ghalib), 44–45; "Ghazal"
     (Haag), 58; "Ghazal I" (Agha),
     53–57; "Ghazals (Homage to
     Ghalib)" (Rich), 43, 46–47, 49;
     Outlyer and Ghazals (Harrison),
     49–50; "Royal" (Stone), 59–60;

"Souvenir" (Hall), 58; *Stilt Jack*
     (Thompson), 53
"Ghazals (Homage to Ghalib)"
     (Rich), 43, 46–47, 49
Ginsberg, Allen, 106
Gioia, Dana, 113–15, 117, 120, 136
Giotto, 4
Gizzi, Peter, 136
"Glanmore Sonnets" (Heaney),
     69–71
Gleick, James, 4–5
Going Forth by Day (Viola), 4–5
Gornick, Vivian, 62, 63
Graham, Jorie, 8
Great Depression (ca.1929–32), 14, 19,
     20, 22–23
Greeting, The (Viola), 4
Gunn, Thom, 92–96, 127, 136
Gwynn, R. S., 115

Haag, John, 58
Hacker, Marilyn, 11, 15, 20, 63, 72,
     80–85, 93
Haitian crises, 33
Hall, Daniel, 58
Harlem Renaissance, 13
Harrison, Jim, 49–51
Harrison, Tony, 73
Hass, Robert, 102
Hayden, Robert, 112
Heaney, Seamus, 15, 20, 69–71
"Hearing of harvests rotting in the
     valleys" (Auden), 19, 22–24, 38
Hecht, Anthony, 20, 25–34, 105
Hejinian, Lyn, 16
Henderson, Stephen, 52
Herbert, George, 85
"Here in Katmandu" (Justice), 25,
     34–36, 38–41
heroic couplets, 6, 7, 15, 87–104; in
     contemporary culture, 89, 91,
     97–98; history of, 88; language
     idioms in, 103; as public

heroic couplets (*continued*)
discourse, 95; structure of, 94–98; *Poems discussed:* "Bedbug" (Phillip), 104; *The Changing Light at Sandover* (Merrill), 93; "Lament" (Gunn), 92–96, 136; "A Satire Against Mankind" (Rochester), 100, 104; "The Spoiler's Return" (Walcott), 92, 99–104, 136; "To My Friend G. N. from Wrest" (Carew), 96–97; "The Yaddo Letter" (Mahon), 92, 96–98
Hillary, Edmund, 34–36, 41
Hix, H. L., 128–31, 135–37
Hollander, John, 63, 82–83
Holocaust, 27–31, 33–34
Homan, Margaret, 67, 69
Honey in the Rock (Tartt), 129
Hours, The (Cunningham), 63
Howe, Susan, 8
Hughes, Langston, 107, 111
Hulme, T. E., 66
hymn meter, 110, 113

iambic pentameter, 3, 7, 111, 130, 134–35
"I Can't Keep up with You" (Waldrop), 106–7
"If We Must Die" (McKay), 11–14
"In a Prominent Bar in Secaucus One Day" (Kennedy), 109
"I Substitute for the Dead Lecturer" (Baraka), 48

Jauss, David, 37
jazz forms, 13
John Henry Days (Whitehead), 111
Johnson, James Weldon, 13
Johnson, Samuel, 68
Jones, LeRoi. *See* Baraka, Imamu Amiri

Justice, Donald, 8–9, 20, 25, 34–41, 124, 140n.13
"Just Real, The" (Moxley), 134–35

Kanda, K. C., 45
Keats, John, 83–84, 109
Keller, Lynn, 148n.6
Kennedy, Dorothy, 105
Kennedy, X. J., 105, 109
Kittredge, George, 123
Kundera, Milan, 4

"Lament" (Gunn), 92–96, 136
L=A=N=G=U=A=G=E Writing, 10, 120, 131–32, 135
Lawler, Justus George, 83–84
Lehman, David, 91
Levertov, Denise, 53
Levi, Primo, 5
Levine, Philip, 127
Lifton, Robert Jay, 30–31
Light, Kate, 68–69
Lodge, Henry Cabot, Jr., 11
Longenbach, James, 99, 141n.17
Look of Things, The (Cole), 63
Love, Death, and the Changing of the Seasons (Hacker), 63, 80–85
love literature, 9, 15, 61–66, 72. *See also* sonnets
Lowell, Robert, 25, 99

Mahon, Derek, 92, 96–98
"Mantis" (Zukofsky), 19, 20
Markusen, Eric, 30–31
Martin, Charles, 105
"Mary's Lamb" (nursery rhyme), 123
Massachusetts Museum of Contemporary Art, 6, 8
McCord, Andrew, 44
McHugh, Heather, 59
McKay, Claude, 11–14
Merrill, James, 20, 63, 93

Merwin, W. S., 20, 43
"Mesmerism" (Cole), 77–80
Milton, John, 68
"A Miracle for Breakfast" (Bishop),
    17–25
Modernism, 66, 135
Moly (Gunn), 127
Morris, Tracie, 108
Moxley, Jennifer, 132–36
music, 91, 106, 108–9

Nelson, Cary, 10
Nelson, Marilyn, 5, 15, 113, 115–20,
    122
New Formalism, 3, 10, 63, 105–6,
    121–22, 131, 135
Nims, John Frederick, 20
"North and South" (Walcott), 99, 102
novels, 4, 62, 63, 65–66
nursery rhymes, 123–24
Nussbaum, Felicity, 90

"Of Being Numerous" (Oppen), 133,
    136
Oppen, George, 127, 133, 136
Oppenheimer, Paul, 64
"Orders of Magnitude" (Hix), 128–31
orientalism, 44, 46
Other Man Was Me, The (Campo),
    63
otherness, triangulation of, 49–50,
    57, 59
Outlyer and Ghazals (Harrison),
    49–50

pantoums, 16
"Parsley" (Dove), 33
patronage, poems of, 96, 98
Patterson, James T., 43
"Paysage Moralisé" (Auden), 23
pentameter. *See* iambic pentameter
Pequigney, Joseph, 71

Percy, Thomas, 110
Perelman, Bob, 132, 136
performance of poetry, 108–11, 120, 125
Perloff, Marjorie, 10, 40, 63, 103
Petrarch, 19, 29, 32, 62, 65
Phillip, Theophilus, 104
Piper, William Bowman, 95
Plath, Sylvia, 87
"Poems from the Margins of Thom
    Gunn's *Moly*" (Duncan), 127
"poetry wars," 3–4, 10, 15, 25, 90,
    105–6, 127–28, 136
politics of form, 10–11, 14, 44, 63, 72,
    141n.17
Pontormo, Jacopo, 4
Pope, Alexander, 88, 92
Porter, Roy, 89
postmodernism, 4–5, 61, 131
Pound, Ezra, 19, 38, 66, 92
Pre-Raphaelite poets, 20
public discourse, 95, 113
puns, 56–57, 74

queer theory, 9, 15, 63–64, 71–73, 92

racial segregation, 107
Rainey, Ma, 51
Randall, Dudley, 112–13
Ransom, John Crowe, 72
rap music, 91, 108
Rich, Adrienne, 6, 14–15, 43–49,
    51–53, 57
Richman, Robert, 37, 106
Richter, David H., 71
"Rivulets of the Dead Jew"
    (Bernstein), 120–25
Rochester, John Wilmot, 2nd earl of,
    100, 104
Rossetti, Christina, 67
Rougemont, Denis de, 64
"Royal" (Stone), 59–60
Rukeyser, Muriel, 123

"Safe Sex" (Campo), 73–77
Said, Edward, 55, 56, 58
Saintsbury, George, 89
"Satire Against Mankind, A"
    (Rochester), 100, 104
Schafer, R. Murray, 107–8
Schnackenberg, Gjertrud, 105
scholarly writing, 15, 90
"School of Eloquence, The"
    (Harrison), 73
Scrovegni Chapel (Padua), 4
Sedgwick, Eve Kosofsky, 71, 72
"Sestina: Altaforte" (Pound), 19
"Sestina d'Inverno" (Hecht), 27–28
sestinas, 6, 14, 15, 17–41; critical
    respect for, lack of, 24–25, 37;
    history of, 19–20, 29; popularity
    of, 20, 22, 24; structure of, 18, 21,
    23, 26–27, 32, 39–40, 53; *Poems
    discussed:* "The Book of Yolek"
    (Hecht), 25–32, 34; "Hearing of
    harvests rotting in the valleys"
    (Auden), 19, 22–24, 38; "Here in
    Katmandu" (Justice), 25, 34–36,
    38–41; "Mantis" (Zukovsky), 19,
    20; "A Miracle for Breakfast"
    (Bishop), 17–25; "Sestina:
    Altaforte" (Pound), 19; "Sestina
    d'Inverno" (Hecht), 27–28;
    "Sestine 5" (Barnes), 19; "Ye
    goatherd gods" (Sidney), 19,
    22, 38
"Sestine 5" (Barnes), 19
Seven Types of Ambiguity (Empson),
    21–22
sexual strength, 50
Shakespeare, William, 65, 68, 71–72
Sheppard, Matthew, 80
Sidney, Philip, 19, 22, 29, 38; "Ye
    goatherd gods," 19, 22, 38
Silliman, Ron, 135
Singer, Irving, 70
Solomon, Jack, 129

Solomon, Olivia, 129
sonnets, 6, 7, 10–14, 61–85; as
    "American" form, 11; feminist
    criticism of, 66–69; gay/lesbian
    revival of, 9, 15, 62–63, 72;
    history of, 64–68, 85, 91;
    language idioms in, 73–74;
    Miltonian, 68, 73; modernist
    criticism of, 66; performance
    and, 111; Petrarchan, 62, 65,
    67, 69–70, 74, 79, 83–84,
    106; postmodernism and,
    61; Shakespearean, 12, 68,
    71–73, 75, 81, 84; structure
    of, 12–13, 64, 75–77, 81–84;
    themes/tropes of, 64–66, 70,
    74, 79–80; *Poems discussed:*
    "About Sonnets of Love; Some"
    (Light), 68–69; "Arte Povera"
    (Cole), 78; "Batter my heart,
    three-personed God" (Donne),
    79; "Glanmore Sonnets"
    (Heaney), 69–71; "If We Must
    Die" (McKay), 11–14; *Love,
    Death, and the Changing of
    the Seasons* (Hacker), 80–85;
    "Mesmerism" (Cole), 77–80;
    "Safe Sex" (Campo), 73–77;
    "Sonnet 130" (Shakespeare), 65
"Sonnet 130" (Shakespeare), 65
soundscapes, 107–8
"Souvenir" (Hall), 58
Spenser, Edmund, 29
Spiller, Michael R. G., 150n.20
"Spoiler's Return, The" (Walcott), 92,
    99–104, 136
Stafford, William, 43
Steele, Timothy, 63–64, 105
Steevens, George, 68
Steiner, George, 29, 34
Stern, Gerald, 10–11
Stewart, Susan, 117
Stilt Jack (Thompson), 53

Stone, Carole, 59–60
Stone, Lawrence, 65
Strand, Mark, 43
Strong Measures (Dacey and Jauss), 37
Sullivan, James D., 113
"Summer Storm" (Gioia), 113–15, 117, 120
Surrey, Henry Howard, earl of, 65

Tartt, Ruby Pickens, 129
Tenzing Norgay, 34–36
Thompson, John, 53
Tolson, Melvin B., 11, 14, 112
"To My Friend G. N. from Wrest" (Carew), 96–97
Trethewey, Natasha, 115

Vendler, Helen, 33
Vietnam War, 45–46
villanelles, 16
Viola, Bill, 4–5
Visible Man, The (Cole), 63

Visitation, The (Pontormo), 4
"Visits to St. Elizabeths" (Bishop), 124

Walcott, Derek, 15–16, 92, 99, 102–4, 136
Waldrop, Rosmarie, 106–7
Weinberger, Eliot, 144n.21
Wellburn, Ron, 52
What the Body Told (Campo), 63, 73
Whitehead, Colson, 111
Wilbur, Richard, 26, 37, 78, 105
Williams, William Carlos, 10, 64, 66
Williamson, Greg, 128
Woolf, Virginia, 71
Wordsworth, William, 87, 110
Wyatt, Thomas, 65

"Yaddo Letter, The" (Mahon), 92, 96–98
Yeats, William Butler, 71

Zukofsky, Louis, 19, 20